RESTLESS
IN THE **CITY**

Thank you for choosing a SAGE product!
If you have any comment, observation or feedback,
I would like to personally hear from you.

Please write to me at **contactceo@sagepub.in**

Vivek Mehra, Managing Director and CEO, SAGE India.

Bulk Sales

SAGE India offers special discounts
for purchase of books in bulk.
We also make available special imprints
and excerpts from our books on demand.

For orders and enquiries, write to us at

Marketing Department
SAGE Publications India Pvt Ltd
B1/I-1, Mohan Cooperative Industrial Area
Mathura Road, Post Bag 7
New Delhi 110044, India

E-mail us at **marketing@sagepub.in**

Subscribe to our mailing list
Write to **marketing@sagepub.in**

This book is also available as an e-book.

RESTLESS
IN THE CITY

Conversations with Young People
in Resettlement Colonies

NIRANTAR

Los Angeles | London | New Delhi
Singapore | Washington DC | Melbourne

First published in 2021 by

SAGE Publications India Pvt Ltd
B1/I-1 Mohan Cooperative Industrial Area
Mathura Road, New Delhi 110 044, India
www.sagepub.in

SAGE Publications Inc
2455 Teller Road
Thousand Oaks, California 91320, USA

SAGE Publications Ltd
1 Oliver's Yard, 55 City Road
London EC1Y 1SP, United Kingdom

SAGE Publications Asia-Pacific Pte Ltd
18 Cross Street #10-10/11/12
China Square Central
Singapore 048423

YODA Press
79, Gulmohar Enclave
New Delhi 110049
www.yodapress.co.in

Published by Vivek Mehra for SAGE Publications India Pvt Ltd. Typeset in 11.5/15pt Adobe Caslon Pro by Fidus Design Pvt Ltd, Chandigarh.

Library of Congress Control Number: 2020950806

ISBN: 978-93-5388-724-7 (HB)

SAGE YODA Team: Amrita Dutta, Neena Ganjoo, Arpita Das, Ishita Gupta and Tanya Singh
Cover Design: Ishita Gupta

Contents

Research Team
Ekta Oza and Sonam Grover

Principle Research Advisor
Sarada Balgopalan

Report Writing
Ekta Oza, Sonam Grover

Report Conceptualization and Special Editing
Archana Dwivedi

Editor
Anita Vasudeva

Research Supported by
Human Capability Foundation, UK

Preface and Acknowledgements

According to the Census data of India 2011, India is a young nation. The data shows that most of the population also lies between the age group that is considered to be 'working'; therefore, the dependency ratio is low. This is marked as a demographic dividend, which is currently an important factor while talking about new policies and the government's new initiatives. Demographic dividend implies that India will benefit from its large young population as the country will have a lot of workers who contribute to the GDP and grow the economy in the process (AICAR Business School 2015).

There is another side to this story. It is true that, for the most part, India's population comprises young people who are a great workforce and this can impact the GDP of the country. This creates high expectations, but there is also a sharp increase in unemployment. In a microcosm, this was adequately reflected by the participants of the present research.

The expectations are high, one, because of the presence of consumer culture and media in daily life, and second, because young people are reaching higher levels of education. However, there are not enough jobs and opportunities available that can meet their aspirations. Living in a resettlement colony exacerbates such a situation as informal slum settlements have long represented a lack of full citizenship. People here exchange votes for the most basic of needs like water and sanitation, and eviction proceeds on highly unequal terms. Keeping these conditions in mind, the present research was conducted by Nirantar to study the issues of friendship, education, migration, violence and family among young people in two resettlement colonies in Delhi.

While discussing the role of the state in the lives of the participants of the present research and how the participants understand the state, we are arguing that the state's idea of illegality and legitimacy is dynamic; it changes with a change in political party, spatial locations and socio-economic status of the particular community. People living in these resettlement colonies have had to negotiate at every step of their subsistence due to the structural exclusion from rights and services, with different actors at play including the law and state. Despite the persistence of enormous difficulties, these boys and girls are very hopeful for their future. They believe that their education can help them alter their socio-economic marginalization, which in turn will allow them to reside in other parts of the city giving them the socio-economic upward mobility that they aspire to.

This marginalization is experienced differently by the boys who yearn to create a different form of masculinity—not disciplined manhood, but an aggressive, uncontrolled masculinity. By actively disengaging from the marginalized pockets of the city, the state and police perpetuate the structural violence. Having worked hard to reach college, but unable to achieve employment, these boys continue to spiral downwards in the vicious cycle of poverty, lack of opportunities, state apathy and continued marginalization. While some boys choose violence as a way to deal with their wounded masculinity, some don't. The vulnerability and fears of the latter, who choose not to, has also been highlighted in the present volume.

This research that went into the making of this book has also been an exploration of the complex relationships that the young boys and girls living in Sanjay Camp and Dakshinpuri have with the various stakeholders who impact their lives in different ways—such as friends, family, social media, the education system and the sarkaar. Narratives of love and friendships shared by boys and girls collude and intermingle to bring forth ideas that cannot be clearly differentiated. There is neither one simple definition of love or friendship, nor a homogenous experience of either. As the research documentation makes clear, both boys and girls experience intimacy in their friendships, but quite differently.

Female friendships revolve around sharing personal narratives of struggles and finding solace in knowing that you are not alone in that struggle, whereas boys find closeness with each other by networking, especially for employment opportunities and monetary help. Since both groups shared their experiences of living in a controlled environment, they had few spaces to interact with peers and form new relationships. Schools, tuition centres and participation in activities organized by the local NGO provide the only spaces where these fleeting moments of interaction, permissible yet controlled, are available to them. Friendships that brew here could then be continued outside in public spaces like parks and malls where they 'cannot be seen' by others who may report it to their families.

From the idea that love is eternal to establishing that there is one and only one true love (*sacha pyaar*) and even further, to how love demands a performance of the normative roles of femininity and masculinity, Bollywood is, for our participants, undeniably the one source of information that defines and dictates how to behave in their friendships and romantic relationships. Both, boys and girls, fantasize about their future love/spouse, but their expectations are often in direct conflict with each other. While girls expect someone who can free them from their present realities, what the boys expect from women generally represent a typical gender stereotype.

One of the aspects that was carefully observed and documented in the research was how both groups feel the impact of patriarchy. While girls could recognize and reflect on their burdens, they imagine the possibility of living their lives differently. The boys' narratives were riddled with the burden of continuing the family lineage, responsibility of procreation and providing for one's family. They, however, lacked the structural reflections which were present in the narratives of the girls, and hence didn't move away from their reality of patriarchy and masculinity to a different imagined aspiration.

At the end, and most interestingly for our purposes, both, boys and girls, wished that co-education would be made mandatory by the government so that schools could provide a safe space where girls and boys would not hesitate to talk nor be scared of each other. The participants felt that this would help in building an understanding of the self and the other that would gradually change the prejudices they harboured against each other.

We would like to first and foremost thank our research participants for taking the time to meet us consistently over the year, for trusting us and sharing their life journeys and their moments of vulnerability with us, and in so doing, also compelling us to reflect on ourselves. Without the honesty and willingness of each one of them to open up to us, this research would have been meaningless.

We would like to express our deep gratitude to our Research Adviser, Sarada Balagopalan, who has been there with us from the inception of the research to the finalization of the report. She guided us throughout our work, from helping us find material for the literature review, to framing the focus group and interview questions to enabling us to be more reflexive as researchers and question our own biases. She always encouraged us with her appreciation and by sharing critical feedback on our writing.

We would like to thank Soni ji, who is the coordinator of the Action India Centre at Dakshinpuri and Sanjay Camp, for introducing us to the participants, and for her unflinching support in helping us coordinate with them. The conversations we had with Soni ji and Krishna ji over cups of tea and lunch made us feel more comfortable in our research site and allowed for a deeper understanding of the context of our work.

Lastly, and most importantly, we would like to thank the internal review team of Nirantar made up of Archana Dwivedi, Prarthana Thakur and Disha Sethi for their feedback on our report which was extremely helpful in making our writing more nuanced, which might otherwise not have happened. Thank you all for contributing to this research which we hope will add to the existing knowledge and understanding of young people in urban resettlement spaces.

Introduction

This volume is the result of Nirantar's work in the two resettlement colonies of Khanpur and Trilokpuri under the project titled PACE (Parvaaz Adolescent Centre for Education). The aim of the project was to work on education with girls who were in the age group of 14 to 25 years and who had dropped out of school. Around the end of the first year of the project, we began to feel the vital need to study issues such as friendship, education, migration, violence and family more thoroughly. With this germinated the concept of this research.

We shared the research concept with Action India, an NGO that has been working for over 20 years in Sanjay Camp and Dakshinpuri and who had also been our partner for the PACE project for two years by then. Our research participants thus included the girls and boys who had been involved in the various activities that are organized by Action India in these resettlement colonies.

The decision to include boys in this research also took shape during our work with PACE, where the high visibility of boys in public spaces created some discomfort for girls, and where brothers of girls voiced their desire to be included in the programme.

We were aware that the result of working with boys in the research project would be twofold: while, at Nirantar, including boys in the research would add to our already layered knowledge of gender and sexuality, in the larger discourse, especially in the development sector in South Asia, it would shine light on both the possibility and the rationale for the need to work with both girls and boys in similar research projects.

Objectives of the Research

The research aimed to probe, explore and deepen the understanding of young people and their lives in resettlement colonies in India's capital in relation to their location and realities. Our objectives for this research are captured most accurately in the following questions that emerged as we began the project: How do young people respond to their lived realities in these resettlement colonies influenced as they are by their class, caste and gender? How are their aspirations and relationships conflicted by the life and society of their highly urbanized, wealthy and consumerist neighbours and the rest of the city?

What impact does this everyday conflict and its resolution have on the lives of young people?

What is the role of the state in creating and perpetuating this conflict, and how does that link with young aspirations?

What do the linkages of caste, class and gender have on the relationships/friendships, love life and idea of marriage amongst young people?

The Methodology

The research methodology included Focus Group Discussions (FGDs) on five themes: namely, state-citizenship, education, work, love-friendship-marriage, and media.

These FGDs were conducted separately with girls and boys, strategically keeping in mind the discourse around mixed-sex interactions particular to this area.[1] After 34 FGDs in total, we conducted two rounds of in-depth personal interviews, which focused on how these themes affect the structural and personal realities of the participants. We included the two sub-themes of caste and violence in the interview questions as these had emerged quite powerfully during the FGDs. The interviews allowed us to get a closer glimpse of the lives of these young people, their aspirations and struggles. We hope the vignettes we share in each chapter do justice to the moments of trust and vulnerability shared between us. The detailed interviews have been made available in the annexures at the end of the book for interested readers and researchers. We also used theatre activities at strategic points when we felt it would help in developing a rapport with the participants, for instance, the first time when we met the group, or in situations where we felt conversations were seeming inhibited, such as during the FGD on love.

Apart from the FGDs, in-depth personal interviews and theatre, we also used drawing as a methodology to share experiences.

Where are we located in this story?

The principles of subjectivity and reflexivity have been central to the method of analysis, where the positioning of the researcher and her experiences form a central point that affects the entire research process from its inception to its final analysis and

---

[1] This has been discussed in detail in Chapters 3 and 4.

outcomes. While we were thinking through the questions on which we would base our discussion on the theme of work, we were reminded by our Advisor, Sarada Balagopalan, of our own biases, where we privilege working women and hence make invisible the double exploitation, economic and domestic, that many women face. This questioned the very ethics of how we, as privileged, middle-class, privately educated 'researchers' feel entitled enough to work with a group of people who lived in a space different from ours, extract knowledge from them, add to the discourse and leave the field having collated the information we had arrived there to acquire. Another aspect that we had to think through with greater focus and clarity was understanding of masculinity. When boys shared their aspirations that included dreams of travelling to America or buying big cars, we judged their masculinity. But when girls shared similar narratives, we were proud of them, ignoring then the connection between consumption and masculinity.

We thus earmarked certain questions for ourselves as well as we began our work with the communities:

Would we conduct a similar research in Chittaranjan Park or Mukherjee Nagar, places where we live?

How mindful were we about opening up life narratives that some of them had managed to either forget or had resolved and moved on?

What did we find strange about their curiosity about our lives (after all we had initiated this curiosity by marching into their lives)?

Informed by feminist research methodology, we decided to both share yet restrict the information we shared. We were nervous about working with boys, although we had experience of working with girls from previous projects. As it turned out, there was no need for a separate strategy; our biases were what we have always had to work through. And yet, we came together, them and us. The popular joke was, 'Oh now Didi is going to ask us "why" do you feel so?'

In psychoanalytic framework of practising therapy, it is believed that we all know the answers to our own questions; what we need is a facilitating and safe environment where this process can be contained. So, we asked the participants, 'Why do you come here regularly?' They responded; 'No one has ever asked us questions about what we think and feel, especially around love and marriage. I get to know what others around me are thinking. I get to know a little more about myself.' That was satisfying.

Locating the Study

In New Delhi, there are a total of 1,650 illegal or unauthorized colonies that house a population of 50 lakh[2] people. The capital of India is inhabited by many people who have migrated from various parts of the country, and have settled, or were re-settled here. Some resettlement colonies like Govindpuri in South Delhi are home to refugees who came from Bangladesh while others like the Walled City or Shahjahanabad, that was declared a slum in 1962, is home to 3.25 lakh people, most of whom have come from the neighbouring state of Uttar Pradesh (see Annexure 1 for the districts of Delhi) (Sultan, 2018).

Out of the 55 resettlement colonies in Delhi, 44 were established between 1960 and 1985. A population of 12 lakh lives in

---

[2] One lakh = one hundred thousand.

the 44 colonies which were established before 1985, and there is no official estimate available of the population that lives in the 11 sites that were created post 2010 (Jeelani, 2018).

Dakshinpuri is a resettlement colony that falls in the first category. It was built in the 1970s when residents from the *Jhugi Jhompri* (JJ)[3] clusters in upscale Chanakyapuri, with its embassies, high commissions and international diplomatic community, were resettled here. Sanjay Camp on the other hand is a JJ Colony.

Dakshinpuri and Sanjay Camp are both situated in Ambedkar Nagar. The very geographic location of the area exemplifies its socio-economic standing in the city: situated in a highly developed part of the city, South Delhi, it is surrounded by luxurious shopping malls such as the Select Citywalk Mall and the DLF Place Mall, and the affluent and sprawling residential localities of Saket and Sainik Farms. The co-existence, uncomfortable and yet symbiotic, of these two kinds of localities exemplifies the paradox of urban development in a South Asian city like Delhi, where a population of approximately 2,17,000[4] lives in a compact and dense housing system, on a small piece of land near expensive homes and modern complexes. The concomitant disparity in the distribution of resources of land, water and electricity is too stark to be ignored.

> *'My mother used to tell me how quiet and empty this place used to be in the beginning. Back then you could count the number of houses that were there, 10–15! It was worth living here in those days. Gradually it became a slum area. This is*

---

[3] Squatter/slum settlements; could be made of mud or any material available.
[4] As shared by the local NGO working in the area, 2 lakh people live in Dakshinpuri and 17,000 in Sanjay Camp.

what people do, they come, set up four walls, then slowly a roof comes on the top and it becomes a house. Now you can see little children roaming around with pistols in their hands. When we were young, we didn't know anything about guns. We used to play with dolls. I used to think katta meant a jute sack; now I know it is slang for an Indian made pistol.

What about the police? They don't use the power they have. They are either scared of the goons here or are corrupt. The government is just busy in advertising for itself, India as a brand. Very few are able to progress in this system. The rich are getting richer and the poor are getting poorer. If there is a demolition here, we should be allotted Delhi Development Authority (DDA) flats. We also pay tax! There are no proper services provided here. if we live in flats, the government might pay attention to us and our needs.'

Rohini, 20 years

The Restructuring of Geographies

There is a difference in the ways in which the various resettlement colonies in Delhi came into being. Both Sanjay Camp and Dakshinpuri came into existence around the time of the emergency when Delhi's map was restructured most drastically (Bhan, 2016). In contrast with other resettlement colonies with histories of communal violence that have led to their emergence, like Welcome in Seemapuri (Tarlo, 2000) that has witnessed communal riots between Hindus and Muslims and Hindus and Sikhs, or settlements near factories like Ghazipuram (Snell-Rood, 2015), or resettlements post the Commonwealth Games of 2010 that created the last batch of resettlement colonies in Delhi, Dakshinpuri and Sanjay Camp don't have a history of communal violence that led to their emergence.

Welcome colony was built after the people who were living on the banks of the Yamuna river were displaced and relocated here. It grew during the infamous sterilization drive initiated by Sanjay Gandhi. The government in his time incentivized its employees in accordance with the targets they achieved in terms of the number of men they could convince to get sterilized. Hence promotions, across all departments, were premised on achieving the highest target. In turn, government employees, across all departments, promised the residents of this newly created resettlement colony of Welcome, that their unauthorized houses would be converted into authorized ones. While thousands of men got sterilized, the promise made by the government never materialized. It is also in this period, that residents realized that they could sell their land, even if it was unauthorized, to make a profit. This led to the mushrooming of settlements across Seelampur (Tarlo, 2000). The Commonwealth Games of 2010 was the next period of notorious land acquisition and sanitization of the streets under the brand of 'smart city' where people living on the streets, people living near the newly built world-class stadiums, and dogs, were forcibly removed and relocated to 11 sites in north, north-west and west Delhi (Jeelani, 2018). While the Commonwealth Games had no direct impact on Dakshinpuri or Sanjay Camp, it changed the geography of Delhi through the acts of demolition and reallocation of settlements carried out across the capital.

Young People, State and Citizenship

Legitimacy

Are you legitimate? How long can you live here?

With a population of 17,000, living in approximately 5,000 *jhuggis*, Sanjay Camp, which was established in 1975, is visually reminiscent of a 'slum' area. It is often described as a space which has been illegally captured by the people, *'ghera hua'*.

The people who lived here were given 'tokens' under the V.P. Singh government (1989–1990), and gradually ration cards, electricity meters and electoral cards too; these documents show that the government recognizes them as real citizens like others whose tenure in Delhi is secure. It is important to note, however, that not everybody has a token. The token is an important document as it ensures that if and when the government orders a demolition here, those who have a token will be rehabilitated elsewhere, while the rest will not be provided with any such alternative. The plots the ones with the tokens will be assigned

will be on the outskirts of the city and will be of a bare minimum 108 sq. ft area. The confusion over the status of Sanjay Camp reflects in the words the participants chose to describe it, which range from *basti* or settlement to a JJ colony.[1]

Dakshinpuri, on the other hand, is a 'legitimate' resettlement colony, which was formed when people were relocated here from the slums near Chanakyapuri and Talkatora during Indira Gandhi's first tenure as Prime Minister (1966–77). The allocation of plots was done by the DDA and people bought these plots for 100 rupees in exchange for official receipts on a lease of 99 years. With a population of 2 lakh, facilities like water pipelines and sewers existed almost since its inception in the 1980s. We have chosen to use the term 'legitimate' to describe Dakshinpuri after Bhan's (2016) use of the same term,

> I use the term legitimate to describe settlements that enjoy a de facto or de jure security of tenure. I mean by this that they are protected – either explicitly within the Plan or implicitly in actual urban development practice – from arbitrary eviction. Settlements that are legitimate need not, therefore, derive their legitimacy only from law (although some can and do).

People came to Sanjay Camp and Dakshinpuri with tarpaulin and bed sheets. Sentiments such as 'this wasn't a place worth living in, people have built it on their own' were shared by each participant during their individual interviews.

[1] Gautam Bhan (2016) in his work based in New Delhi explains on understanding the politics behind labelling places of residence, like slums/settlement colonies/authorized colonies, etc.: 'Slum designated areas are protected from arbitrary eviction without resettlement and thereby enjoy a certain de facto security of tenure though not a de jure one'(p. 73).

This expression of changing the urban landscape with their histories of migration is found in the narratives of people living in different resettlement colonies across Delhi.[2]

Dakshinpuri has transformed now from *kuchha*[3] houses to *pucca*[4] ones with brick and cement, while Sanjay Camp still has many *kuchha* houses and is thus described either as an 'unauthorized *basti*' or a *jhuggi jhompri* by the people. Afsana eloquently described the difference by saying, 'This is Sanjay "Camp", camp; and that is Dakshinpuri.' The term 'camp' here signifies a sense of constant shifting or impermanence. The property rates are higher in Dakshinpuri as compared to those in Sanjay Camp; Dakshinpuri is located in South Delhi and has all the expected civic amenities such as clinics, schools, markets, and so on.

Infrastructure for the Citizen

Dakshinpuri is marked by a park at the entrance that has an open gym and where the nearby residents go for walks. In contrast, Sanjay Camp has a park that is either littered with garbage or is used as a space to rear pigs; it is also referred to as the 'non-veg' park. The third park in the area is the Jahanpanah forest or the 'jungle park' as the participants like to refer to it, which connects both settlements, Dakshinpuri and Sanjay Camp, to the nearby affluent colonies of Alaknanda and Greater Kailash.

---

[2] Snell-Rood (2015) in her work on understanding the lives of women living in Ghazipuram, a Delhi slum, explains, 'However, while residents came at different points of their life and at different moments in Delhi's development over a twenty-year period, in all of their stories, residents emphasized how they built a place in this city – both literally, through the settlements they established, and through their work, which connected them to the larger outside world'(p. 139).

[3] Houses made of mud and tin roofs, symbolizing impermanence.

[4] Houses made of brick and cement, symbolizing permanence.

It is in this park that friends and lovers from the settlements find moments of undisturbed intimacy.

As far as health services go, the closest private hospitals are Batra and Max in Saket. Batra has a government wing where the BPL card is supposed to provide access to free treatment, but what happens in reality is a little more complicated. The closest government hospital is in Malviya Nagar. There are two or three dispensaries in Dakshinpuri but none inside Sanjay Camp. There are many private clinics here, but only two of these have doctors who have a verified degree. The Mohalla Clinic, a scheme introduced by the current Delhi state government after 2016, is a medical service in a mobile van that comes to the locality every Thursday. The van comes equipped with three to four doctors and one can procure all kinds of medicines from them. While it is not a free service, one need only pay a minimum of 20 rupees to access it.

There are two ration shops in Dakshinpuri and one inside Sanjay Camp. There are no banks in either of the two places; the closest ones are in Khanpur and Madangiri. But there are around seven to eight ATMs in Dakshinpuri. Everyone in the locality has a bank account either in the State Bank of India or in Canara Bank, while some of the participants' parents have accounts in the nearby Post Office as well. There is only one police station here, which is in Virat. The next closest one is located at Tara Apartments in the upmarket South Delhi locality of Alaknanda. CCTV cameras have been installed by the people in Dakshinpuri and hence, they pay for their repair and maintenance. There are two CCTV cameras installed by the government at the two toilets in Sanjay Camp. Safety is clearly a concern here. Some of the participants have witnessed people being murdered and shot at. There is a sense of fear among the young residents and their parents too are concerned for their safety.

Varun, who is 19 and has recently given his Class 12 exams, shared hesitatingly, 'I am scared to go out alone, especially at night. When we see 3–4 boys standing in a group I do feel scared.' Some of the boys are not allowed to step outside after 9–10 pm.

Sanjay Camp is a densely packed cluster of houses, two to three floors each, a maze of open drains marking the entrance to each house, and, as you walk down, water drips down on you from the clothes on the clothes-lines hanging high and low.

Televisions are common and some homes have air conditioners as well. With the help of a local NGO that has been working here for a long time, Action India, water pipelines were laid in the locality in 1992, and as recently as two years ago, one public toilet was constructed.

However, the supply of water has been consistent only over the last one or two years, partly due to the constant efforts at negotiation by the residents themselves and their own initiative and partly due to the programme of the new government in Delhi that came to power in 2016. We find, however, that only one of these pipes is connected to the government water supply from Sarita Vihar. The rest of the pipes still use water from borewells. People share water as and when the supply comes, a chore that both young girls and boys are seen taking responsibility for. When supply is short, they must pay and get water tankers, separate for drinking water and separate for other consumption. If there is an issue with the supply of water, they write a complaint letter to the Station House Officer (SHO) at the Nigam Parishad (Councilor).

While Sanjay Camp has an open drainage system, the residents of Dakshinpuri got their sewarage system covered using their own money. 'The Municipal Corporation of Delhi (MCD) people have to be asked to come and clean our sewers in Sanjay Camp. My mother has the number of the MCD official, she calls, and he comes,' informed Ajay, an 18-year-old who studies in Class 12.

In Dakshinpuri, there is a person assigned who collects garbage directly from homes, but in Sanjay Camp the residents must go to the main dumpster to dispose of their garbage. These dumpsters are kept locked and maintained well, but this too is a recent practice.

Electricity hasn't been an issue since the new state government came to power in 2016 as bills have been subsidized since then. Each household has an individual meter; while the residents in Sanjay Camp pay 5 rupees per unit, residents of Dakshinpuri must pay 8 rupees per unit. 'Electricity rarely goes and if it does, it comes back within minutes,' shares Afsana.

There are two public toilets in Sanjay Camp, but one got locked due to non-payment of bills. The girls must pay 1 rupee while the boys 2 rupees to use this public service. The houses in Dakshinpuri have attached bathrooms.

Sarkaar

Before we explore the relationship of these young people with the state, it is important to define the use of the Hindi term 'sarkaar', which the participants have used to denote the term 'government'. The government for them is the collection of representatives of the elected political party, as well as government institutions responsible for providing services, like the Municipal Corporation of Delhi (MCD) and the Delhi Development Authority (DDA). As the participants describe them, these governing bodies work for the people and think about the welfare of their *janta* (people). Their responsibilities as shared by the participants include: giving loans to farmers, providing facilities like electricity and water, keeping the rates of vegetables in control, converting *kuchha* houses into *pucca* ones, building schools, colleges, hospitals, roads, providing transportation facilities, giving scholarships to students, providing pension to government employees, and so on.

'But the government puts a limit on the extent of our rights, like with the Right to Education the age is fixed at 14 years,' was the keen observation by Afsana.

Sarkaar and the Right to Basic Amenities

Earlier there were only jhuggis[5] here. Indira Gandhi's government gave us plots here. First there were tents, slowly walls were built that gave rise to small houses. Since we continued staying here, the pucca houses replaced the kuchha houses. Some houses have two storeys too. But people constructed their own homes, not the government. We get water supply too. My mother used to tell me that earlier they would have to fetch water from tankers or from their neighbours' homes. There have been many changes. The size of the houses is increasing, construction is rampant.".

Prakash, 20 years

[5] A Hindi word that closely resembles a 'slum' in its representation; densely packed houses with narrow lanes, open sewage, and often houses made of mud or tin roofs.

The narrations of the failure of the government to support the people in reconstructing their lives, and the efforts of the people to build their lives from scratch, figured in each and every interview we conducted. What makes this narrative even starker is that the affluent localities of Greater Kailash, Pushp Vihar, Saket, Malviya Nagar, and Sainik Farms that surround them appear in sharp contrast to these two localities with regard to this issue. These upmarket localities have good roads, CCTV cameras for security provided by the city authorities, garbage collection and disposal systems, clean public spaces, transportation services, police protection and well-built houses.

Sonu is 20 years of age and pursuing his BA at an open university. His family was among the first to come to Dakshinpuri and the most affluent in the area. He observes, 'Educated people stay there and the rent is high there. This comes under "local" area and that comes under "standard" area. If people smoke there it becomes their status symbol, but if people smoke here then it becomes a bad habit.'

The list of differences continues,

Many hawkers are not allowed inside these gated communities, there is only one that is allowed to enter.

They are not even dependent on the government. If they don't get electricity, they have generators, or they have links in the electricity department, where one call will suffice and fix everything. They will ask for the power connection to poor households to be cut because they have a meeting to conduct. If one person living in Saket will complain, electricity will be resumed, while here even if ten people complain it will take long.

The participants explain this discrimination further: 'It is because of the area; the electricity department thinks ours is a local area and doesn't require power as its absence would not create difficulties in our lives. But other places need electricity since their bills are also higher.'

The social marginalization, which is based on class and caste in the case of Dakshinpuri and Sanjay Camp, defines much of the discrimination residents have to face. While they face discrimination in gaining access to services like water and electricity, their access to the government for redressal is also impeded, thereby creating another discrimination.

Meena, a 16-year-old girl, studying in Class 12, offers a sharp critique of the state and its failure that also defines the residents' relationship with the state:

There is no relationship with the state! Sarkaar doesn't even see us. But we keep our hope alive that maybe this time things will be corrected. But they never do. We still don't get piped water, it comes from the ground. Our people go from one office to another to lodge a complaint. Maybe the sarkaar sees us but it doesn't want to pay attention to us. Even if we want to speak up we can't because we belong to a small community. We can reach the Counsellor at the most. He will tell us there are more people sitting above him in the hierarchy. Till where can we reach? If we inquire, they say that they have passed on our file! So, the biggest fault is the sarkaar's. Why are they not doing their job properly? Places like Saket are different. This is Sanjay Camp, Camp [she emphasizes by repeating the word]. This is a *jhuggi*. You can observe for yourself, only *jhuggis* are struggling with these issues. This is the biggest problem. Water is supplied to only those places where the rich/powerful (*bade log*) stay.

Meena's harshness stings. However, the evidence of discrimination based on the group one belongs to is there for all to see; in this case the community's location of residence and class decide its negotiating power with the state.

If one were to enquire what lies behind such rampant discrimination it emerges that one aspect of this discrimination is based on the spatial location and 'group-based differentiation' determined by where one lives and the class and caste that one (the community) belongs to. This determines one's access to the state and its services.[6] It is a technique of rule, what Roy (2016: 88) calls 'a spatial mode of governance'.

Perhaps even more importantly, the other aspect is embedded in our Constitution itself: the distinction between the Fundamental Rights which include civil and political rights (such as the right to vote) and the Directive Principles of State Policy which include socio-economic rights (such as those to health, education, shelter). This distinction essentially led to a difference between what would be considered a 'right' and what a 'need'. Hence, basic services such as health and education (which come under the Directive Principles of State Policy) are treated not as entitlements and rights but rather as symbolic of 'what a population needs' and are not guaranteed by the Indian Constitution (Bhan, 2016).

With the promulgation of the Right to Education in 2009, education became a right, but one of its limitations, as also observed by a participant, is its age category that leaves behind

---

[6] Bhan explains this further, 'Group differentiation remains an important mediator in the relationship between the individual and the state. The criteria of what defines a group, therefore, is an important site for the politics of citizenship as categories old and new, established and emergent, seek to access rights, resources and entitlements' (2016, p. 156). As Bhan elaborates, 'the production and regulation of illegality is part of, and not outside, planning and planned development.'

children below age 6 and above age 14. And now with changes to the no-fail policy, the provisions of the right are being diluted further, directly affecting these marginalized youths. Although India is a welfare state, by denying these basic rights of health and shelter, this 'spatial mode of governance' ensures that the marginalized remain at the margins. In the particular case of the localities where we are carrying out research, the constant economic burden of saving money to run households, combined with the architectural flaws of the space lead to acute unwarranted stress.

As Aarti notes,

> They [residents of affluent localities] can get everything delivered to their doorstep. They take their cars for a five-minute distance, and to save five rupees we will have to walk great lengths. We must think about each problem; if we don't get water we have to complain, save money to run our households; there is perpetual tension. They don't have to run around to access these services. Since the lanes are narrow, the ambulance too can't reach us, we must go out on a bike, even late at night.

Their struggles don't end here. Dakshinpuri has the relative security of a 99-year lease, while Sanjay Camp residents still hold on to ration cards, electricity meters, etc., as the only documentation of their right to be where they are. It is because of this fragile claim to citizenship that Sanjay Camp has faced several demolition threats in the past. While on the one hand they keep receiving notifications, on the other, they continue to construct and build homes in the hope that if it is a *pucca* house, demolition might be averted. Notices they periodically receive say that their *jhuggis* will be demolished to build DDA flats.

Zoya shares her anxieties with us:

> For my *jhuggi*, we have complete proof that it belongs to us. We have ration cards, papers to prove that this address belongs to us, we have complete legal documents. If we are displaced from here where will we go? The government says that people who have complete documents will be allotted flats. These flats will be very far from here. Will there be any facilities where we will be shifted? Our livelihood is here, if we are shifted to a far-off place like Narela, we are not going to leave our work and shift there!

Anil, another participant, is a bit more ambivalent about this,

> Yes, we keep getting notices, but nothing has happened so far. I want the demolition to happen. We've been staying in these small houses for long enough. If not a house, at least a plot should be provided. But I don't trust that we'll get either. That is why I am studying. But if demolition does happen, where will so many people go?

This anxiety and the ambivalence about the security of their legal status with regard to housing further impinges upon their sense of belonging to a city.

Voting for Change: Citizenship

One possible explanation for why the demolitions haven't been executed yet is the caste-based electoral process. The huge population that lives in Sanjay Camp are mostly Dalit, forming a substantial chunk of the vote bank.

Anil elaborates, 'If there is a demolition, there are many voters here. The political leader from here will not receive any votes then. Therefore, they never go through with their threats of demolition. Votes are precious to the political leaders; if they get votes only then can they win.'

While the residents here continue to vote in the hope for a change, they are well aware about the political value of their marginalization in the eyes of the local politicians.

Indeed, it is not that they are unaware about or in denial of the political malaise that characterizes democracy in our country. They are sharply conscious and even critical of the same.

After all, it is they who are affected directly by government policies or the absence of the same; the bourgeoisie can afford to lead a life of ignorance. It is then the right to vote that becomes the tool through which they can make themselves heard. The question, of course, is who is listening to them? As shared by the participants, they do know that they are being ignored and invisibilized by the government. Then why do they continue to vote?

'In the hope that something will change. In the hope for a better life, the life we are living in such difficulty would be improved.' This is a sentiment shared by Aarti, Rohini, Varun and most of the other participants.

Some, however, are also disillusioned by this 'democratic' process. 'I will not vote without money because after winning they never once return to look out for us. The best service is around the time of elections. They come for the first 1–2 years, then they forget about us,' concludes Afsana.

In the face of such a reality, the burden of discerning the intentions of the politicians rests with their constituencies, depending on which, they cast their decisive votes (Snell-Rood, 2015, p. 30). For the ones who are younger now and have a year or so to decide whether they will vote or not, the unanimous voice is that they will vote for the choice of their political party in order to ensure 'development of their area'.

Nazrana laments,

I have seen no one takes elections seriously here. Only when it comes to the MCD elections, people start thinking weeks in advance and discuss the issues based on which they would cast their votes. Because MCD is the closest to us, we can complain to them at any point about anything. We motivate others to vote as well then. Like when BJP came to power, Modi had come, and everyone voted for him because his speeches were impressive. But now after demonetization, we don't know who we will vote for. By now people would've understood whether he has benefited us or not.

We hope that if a government comes to power they will do something, therefore we vote. If they work for us, we are happy to vote them back into power again. If they don't, we make sure to not vote for them and bring them down. We don't have a relationship with sarkaar; they come to us for votes and we make them work for us. But the government needs to change because many poor people live in Delhi. Sarkaar doesn't pay attention to them. What about the rich? They live comfortably in any case. They need to bring about changes, provide employment; even those who have graduated don't have job opportunities. Sarkaar thinks that it cannot trust those who are uneducated because they might incur losses to the company or speak differently.

Sandeep, 18 years

Elections have always been fought over *'bijli-paani aur sadak'* (electricity-water and roads), and at some point the increasing rate of vegetables like onions were added to this list (Dugger,

1998). But increasingly we are observing that election campaigns based on the promises of vikaas or development with a focus on capitalizing on the productivity of the youth through claims of skills and employment, are taking centre-stage. But are these promises of development being fulfilled? If so, then who is benefiting and at the cost of whom?

CONCLUSION

In exploring the relationship these young people have with the state, we chose to use Gautam Bhan's framework of analysis in his work, *In the Public's Interest: Evictions, Citizenship and Inequality in Contemporary Delhi* (2016). It must be pointed out, however, that we studied a different population, that is, the 'youth' living in resettlement colonies, who have been far less researched in relation to the question of citizenship.

We explored the role of the *sarkaar* and the influence and infrastructure available to the people here as citizens. What are the aspirations of these young people? What is the role of the state in either bridging the gap between these aspirations and their realities?

Delhi's most famous illegal colony, Sainik Farms, is less than a kilometre away from Sanjay Camp. The residents of Sainik Farms are the affluent and connected people of the city who enjoy access to the services that their counterparts in the illegal settlement of Sanjay Camp are denied.

This unequal distribution of resources is based purely on the difference in the class status of the two, thereby classifying the category they belong to.

This raises the following questions: Is citizenship then defined within a rights-based framework that allows for a possibility of equity or is it based on how the state labels you based on where you live? Could citizenship also be read as a form of belonging, much like the sense of having a home can give you, a sense of safety and permanence?

In a city like Delhi, however, where unplanned growth is in fact the norm of housing and shelter (Bhan, 2016), who is a citizen is defined by the label the state uses to describe you.

Voting, then, performs the visible function through which the state makes its presence felt and the citizens make their voice heard, even if momentarily. As Snell-Rood observes, 'Politicians added to residents' initial investments in neighbourhood infrastructure, knowing that infrastructure served as a visual reminder of their services – and thus encouraged loyalty.'

It is also the politicians' will and decision to act that mattered more than what is written in the law, as is exemplified by the actions of the V.P. Singh government which allotted 'tokens' to the residents of Sanjay Camp as markers of authorized residence. Or the recent symbolic gesture by the current state government of announcing that they will not allow any more demolitions; indeed, governments 'with the intent to do so' have extended their support beyond the realm of the law. But are these symbolic gestures and documents in the form of tokens, electricity bills and ration cards sufficient to facilitate the exercise of one's citizenship?

Their needs still remain basic—free newspaper distribution, electricity, clean drinking water, end to corruption, cleanliness, better quality of education and infrastructure at their schools, de-addiction centres, bathrooms in every house, employment, street lights, parks with swings, security guards and gates, closed drainage system so that during the rains their homes do not get inundated with rainwater, police to be more conscious of their duties, increased patrolling with police cars, hospitals that are closer to access, better transportation services, cheaper cinema halls, and a complaint box through which they can reach out to the government.

The most striking note is communicated in Afsana's exasperation, 'The people who live on rent be given permanent houses from the government. The rich should be removed from the DDA house allotment scheme; this should be only for the poor. What do the rich need it for? The poor are getting poorer and rich richer. My father's salary hasn't increased.'

The promises made to the the residents of these localities by different governments are similar, and yet the gap is too evident to be ignored. Afsana also reminds us what terminologies like 'slum' and 'jhuggi' or in this case 'camp' symbolizing temporariness do to their identity in the eyes of the government. Like the resident status, their citizenship status also becomes temporary. As illegal occupants, their ability to negotiate and claim their entitlements gets diluted.

With the new government in Delhi, the budget for education and health is the highest it has ever been. Government schools are being dedicatedly improved. The mohalla clinics are bridging the gap in the access to health care for these people. Could these recent efforts made by the government to slowly inch towards inclusion by recognizing them as equal citizens, and recognising the hope and aspirations these young people have for their lives, perhaps open new windows to finally claiming citizenship within a rights-based framework? Will these efforts, in the long run, be able to change the 'spatial mode of governance' adequately (Bhan, 2016: 151)? The narratives of the participants seem to communicate their hope that they are slowly becoming visible in the eyes of the new government and their hope that this will continue.

2

Aspirational Education
Elusive Jobs

With formal schooling comes hope as well as a burden of expectations which is placed on the shoulders of these young people: achieving higher qualifications is seen as a way out of poverty.

—Morrow, 2013

Going to malls, posting photographs with friends, buying the latest android phone, travelling to the US or Singapore, buying a house in Gurgaon or Bombay, having a fashion boutique of their own, running one's own business or becoming a famous singer—are some of the many colours and forms of aspirations the young participants of our research project have for their lives. One doesn't have to look beyond Bollywood to understand one of the primary ways in which these aspirations take shape and are moulded further.[1]

---

[1] Kabita Chakraborty talks about young people's perspectives on eve-teasing in her work in the *bastis* of Kolkata thus, 'Bollywood in particular fetishizes middle and upper class Hindu college going youth in contemporary films...Indian youth participating in tertiary schooling, global work opportunities and undertaking greater domestic and international mobility than decades past...this popular

Our participants recognize the importance of being handy with computers and acquiring English-speaking skills in the job market, and hence enrol in coaching centres, if and when they can afford to, to keep working on these skills in the hope of being able to access the employment they desire. But is the gap between their realities and their aspirations too pronounced to be bridged?

The Reality of Lived Lives

The sharings during the FGDs and interviews reveal how the aspirations of the young—filled as they are with dreams of malls and parties, trips to America and Dubai, being independent and respected professionals—clash often with the reality of their everyday life and beliefs. Social conditioning, caste, class, and gender mobility—all these play a role in shaping their lives.

When we asked them who worked where, what they thought they did, these are some of the responses we collated:

> *Boys drink, smoke, get funny with girls; sometimes they get rowdy and show off.*
> *Boys clean roads, cars, sell papers, work as helpers and in shops or garages.*
> *Some of them are tailors, or work in parlours; some even teach dance and computer skills. They'll do electrician's work (mostly married men) or work in small shops that sell momos and chowmein.*
> *They sell liquor too.*

---

imagery of "modern youth," however systematically excludes poor, marginalized, and minority communities in India, further limiting understanding of the variety and richness of different youth cultures across the nation' (2015, p. 5).

> Boys and men clear garbage; they work in bars and clubs, serving or being bartenders.
> They sell water and ice or ice cream at kiosks.
> Better jobs are those of labourers, painters, gym trainers, volunteers for promotion of political parties, and even lawyers or CAs; [some also mentioned] a compounder's job in a clinic or a social worker with an NGO.
> Married men sell vegetables too.
> The men also get the vegetables, and rations and fill the water. The girls do go to school, and work at jobs as well.
> They work in NGOs, as lawyers' assistants, as beauticians and helpers, and in doctor's offices.
> They clean roads and are teachers of computer skills and also give tuitions and might also be air hostesses and singers.
> Girls sell vegetables and momos; one even sells chicken. They sell chowmein and bidis. They wander the streets selling these items or are salesgirls at malls and at Sarojini Market. They work in people's homes, and often take up stitching work. They also make food at schools and distribute the midday meal and do tiffin service.

The girls know that there is a lot of study and training required to be a lawyer (they mentioned five years), a two-month course for a diploma to be a gym trainer, and a three-year BSW from Delhi University or IGNOU to be a social worker. They weren't so sure about the qualifications to become a CA *(commerce for sure)* or about how long it takes to be a doctor (many years, they wondered).

The girls know how to do all the housework, and many agree that they get the men in the house to do some housework too. Ankita says, 'I get my father to do a lot of work, even sweep and swab sometimes.'

Mobility is a real issue for unmarried girls, and affects both education and work. 'Married women have the freedom to go wherever they want and work in other people's homes, or sell vegetables. All sorts of characters land up to buy vegetables and stuff from stalls, so it isn't safe for unmarried girls to do these jobs. But both can work in parlours.'

Education: Government Schools vs Private Schools

The government school system plays a very important role in whether the residents access education in this area or not. While attending the local government school is the norm, being able to go to a private school is the aspiration.

Taj shares with us,

Our English gets better. Good education means a private school. Those who attend private schools become really intelligent. In Sanjay Camp, not many go to private schools, maybe one or two. Mostly they go to government schools. But nowadays boys and girls around us are saying that English is necessary and that our country is becoming digital India, so a few more children have started going to private schools. You know what they say—if you study English from the beginning, then your English gets better. So, they study in private schools till Class 10 and then shift to government schools. They get a solid education till Class 10 and after that they easily get admission in government schools.

Meena's family decided to transfer her brother from a government school to a private one. He used to get beaten up often, and once he grew up a little, he would run away from school and bunk classes.

Comparing private schools with government schools, Nishant says that,

They used to teach with projectors there; everything was taken seriously; homework was given; copies were checked daily. Even after the period was over, the teacher would sit and check the copies. Here, in the government school, if it is checked, then it is checked, otherwise it doesn't matter to anyone. The private school had a machine for drinking water, here there is a tank. There we would get lunch in a canteen, here we get to eat the 'midday meal'.

Mushrooming of Private Coaching Centres

Private schools and tuition centres are mushrooming in the locality. Most private schools are unrecognized and hence they function till only Class 5. The ones that are recognized are Amity International, Gyan Bharti and Delhi Public School, all in Saket. The fee for tuitions is around ₹400–500 per subject, per month. But this increases with higher classes and as exams get nearer; it might even go up to ₹1000–1500 per subject. 'Teachers in private school don't have the required qualification; some of them are just 12th pass. Government school teachers have to study a course and give an entrance exam to qualify to become a teacher,' say the girls as they explain the difference between the two.

The importance of English is recognized by all, whether for getting a better job or to be able to communicate with people 'outside' (the camp?). Similarly, computer skills are imperative to get jobs as data operators or at malls. For boys, driving skills become essential if they want to get hired as delivery boys with private companies. Despite the safety of a government job, no one wants to continue working in the government, even though their fathers might work with the MCD departments, as they aspire to get out of the cycle of doing menial jobs and make use of their years of education.

The seriousness of education in private schools and the emphasis on teaching English are seen as important aspects missing in government schools. In addition to the lack of services, teacher absenteeism is an issue in both girls' and boys' schools. However, an additional reason for worry for the boys is that there no guards at the gates during the boys' shift and the teachers are themselves scared of the boys in case they get violent with them. During the girls' shift, however, attendance is mandatory in every period, and there are two guards each at the two gates of the school. But most importantly, girls fear bunking because if they are caught, which they certainly would be, they would be questioned and might be punished as well.[2] The boys, on the other hand, are not scared, not of being caught loitering about or of being seen by parents or other members of the community outside the school.

There is also a narrative that the government schools have undergone a drastic change in the last 1–2 years. 'They resemble private schools now.' It is reported that there have been improvements in the following ways: CCTV cameras have been installed to monitor teacher absenteeism and prevent students from stealing and bunking; there is supply of clean drinking water; mid-may meals are first checked by the principal and distributed in classrooms under the supervision of teachers; there are now English-medium sections which begin from Class 1 and go up to Class 12; and that the quality of desks and bathrooms and the structures in which the schools are housed have improved.

---

[2] Kabita Chakraborty explains this further: 'Young women's education and employment opportunities have changed over the last decade because of several factors. One factor is many local NGOs and INGOs with a mandate to "educate the girl child" have privileged female education, with some schemes supporting higher studies of females only. This focus on the girl child stems from gendered development concerns in the 1990s which saw the emergence of gendered targets for education participation and completion, as well as support for young women in vocational training and employment schemes, offered by international and state sponsors. Campaigns like the UNICEF International Day of the Girl and the national BetiBachaoBetiPadho campaign aim to close the gender gap in India for girl children in fields such as education and health' (2015, p. 8).

If some of this is indeed a reality, then there is hope that things may still go in the right direction for the next generation.

There's a lot of difference from earlier. Look at my school itself—earlier it was in tents, today there is a full-fledged building with everything, bathrooms, fans, etc. The teachers are also new, the rooms are new. First there were just one or two fans. Now there is a separate tank for water; earlier it was made of mud and sometimes covered, sometimes not. They have installed cameras. In my school all these changes have been introduced, I don't know about others. In our times the studies were okay. However the Principal wanted things handled, the teachers would do it that way. Now the Principal has changed. In three years, the whole map of the school has completely changed. The children stay till the evening to study. It has become disciplined. The Principal says, tell me which teachers are not teaching and I will see to them; now the focus is on the children, if they have a problem, tell me. The good principals and the good teachers get transferred out.

Manoj

Masculinity and Education

One recurrent theme across narratives was that boys do not find any purpose or meaning in schooling, hence they lack the motivation to continue education.

As Nishant puts it,

All the boys over 15, they tell everyone at home that they are going to school, pick up their school bags and off they go to loiter around and smoke cigarettes. The boys who are the studying kind, they manage to study. It's like those girls who are told they can't study, but they want to, so they complete their 12th standard. But the boys who drink and smoke and roam around here and there all the time, they don't even manage to complete the 10th.

Rajesh agrees with this.

Some are in pretty bad condition. They just leave their studies. They manage till the 8th standard, because the government passes you till then irrespective of how you do. After that they don't go to school. Mostly it's the boys who drop out. Studies should be done first, fashion later. If they fail once, they just drop out. Then there are some who get their attendance marked and then spend the rest of the day loitering on the streets. A lot of them just drop out after the 5th or the 8th.

Aman adds,

Can anyone make boys listen to them? Even the parents have no say. Girls are forced to leave school; the parents fear they will get a boyfriend. But boys leave on their own accord, *unka man nahi karta isliye*. Brothers too, many a times, force their sisters to drop out because they feel that now she has grown up and needs to be at home and learn the domestic way of life. Parents also listen to the boys in such cases.

Afsana explained further why boys drop out and girls don't,

There are boys who drop out once they fail a class, usually in the 9th or 10th. Girls still try even if they fail a year. See, when boys fail (she paused), can I tell you honestly? When a girl fails, she is scolded and taunted that she has failed. If we do not try and study now, we won't be able to achieve anything in our lives. It does not bother boys at all. Nobody gives them any attention, even if they are loitering around outside the whole day. When I go looking for my brother, I see so many boys just hanging around. Somebody is hitting someone, someone is running behind a dog. I am sure my brother also does this!

Really, I feel that though we say that boys will cope; once they fail they don't have the inner motivation to try again. There are a few who want to achieve something in life, only they manage to do so. Not the rest.

There are many here who leave school and just sit outside, idle. They have no work either to do. Since her childhood, a girl is told that if she fails she will be restrained to stay at home. This is why I feel no girl fails; compared to the boys fewer number of girls fail.

The unrestricted and unquestioned mobility that boys have traditionally enjoyed solely because they are boys has gradually turned on its head and is costing them their education. What we are attempting to understand here is the link between the privileges that boys have enjoyed under patriarchy, like mobility, and their current loss of the very means to achieve their masculine identities—education to gain employment in order to be able to financially support their families. Girls know that education is that one asset that can bring them closer to their hopes and aspirations of a life without restrictions, and a life on their own terms.

It is telling how gender privilege is actually working against the boys. While girls, who under pressure from their families, and also because of internalized norms of shame and embarrassment, work hard and continue their education, it is very easy for boys to drop out of school and not be embarrassed about it.

Additionally, since schools are the only legitimate reasons for mobility for girls, they strive hard to keep this alive for themselves, but boys do not need this excuse of going to school for their mobility, so there's no commitment to sustaining this relationship.

As a result of all these factors, education as aspiration to change their lived realities still works with the girls while the boys seem to be disillusioned by this.

Thus, the relationship of the boys in these localities with education has changed drastically leading to substantial disengagement and sometimes even a violent retaliation by the boys. The way perceptions of masculinity and the attendant fears play out in the school systems—where teachers and administration are fearful of disciplining the boys but become hyper-vigilant in protecting the sexuality of the girls—has further curtailed the spaces and opportunities for boys to express and live and perform the masculinity of their choosing.

The Case for Co-education Schools

A number of reasons were given by both boys and girls for having co-ed schools were. A most important one was that boys and girls hesitate in front of each other; they don't know how to talk to each other and this would change with co-ed schools. Second, studying together in schools would help the process of understanding each other, which would challenge the prejudices they harboured against each other. However, girls also shared with us that they are scared of boys. They felt that the boys could say anything to them at any time and tease them, and studying together would help them overcome this as it would make it easier to make friends with boys. The boys shared that having co-ed schools would remove the idea that all boys are the same; not everyone does stalking and eve-teasing— they aren't a homogenous category of sexual harassers.

Employment

The gap in being a graduate and still being unemployed is a reality for many young boys in these localities. According to Sandeep, the relationship between the people and the government is only to carry out a transaction, where the government must provide (job/employment) opportunities for the people, thus allowing them to realize their aspirations. When he says that the rich are leading comfortable lives and hence the government needs to focus more on the poor, he is speaking of equity, where the distribution of resources (and opportunities like employment) should be need-based instead of the one-size-fits-all framework.

Sandeep has recently passed his Class 12 exam. He wanted to become a Chartered Accountant (CA) but has had to settle for a Cost Management Accountant (CMA) job since preparing for CA is expensive and requires longer commitment. He also wants to be a model and has had his portfolio photographed in a friend's studio. Many young Dalit boys aspire to become models and a studio photo-shoot, costing between 2000 to 5000 rupees, is a common expense they are willing to undertake.

Throughout his school life Sandeep has participated in theatre and he has also performed during festivals in Sanjay Camp and elsewhere. His most memorable performance was his portrayal of Sita during the Ramayana play which was staged in Virat. Any occasion to dance, even during an ongoing FGD, and he would promptly ask for a dupatta, drape it around himself as a sari and start dancing. While people do tease him for dressing up like a girl, he is least perturbed by their taunts, 'When I'm on the stage, I'm the one performing. They are in the audience! When people clap for me, I feel very nice. My parents are also very supportive.'

Sandeep also understands the realities of living as a boy in this patriarchal structure where the burden of earning and financially supporting one's family is seen as the man's primary role, 'What about the girls? A good match is selected for them and they are married off. Men must support their parents and wives. A boy who doesn't study is married in a small house where the girl too is not educated (*choti jagah*); if the boy is educated the girl will be too.'

The failure of the state to provide employment thus has a much bigger impact on the lives of these young boys and girls whose future rests on their ability to fend for themselves in the absence of any social or economic capital to support their dreams and aspirations.

Having been disillusioned by the government, Shekhar too knows the only way he can change his life and his future is by working hard and planning his present well. He says,

By working with 'Chef Shop' I am going to earn 2.5 lakh and open my own computer coaching centre. I will get the best of the best teachers to teach there. I will charge ₹1000 per month as tuition fee. Even if 60 students will come there per month, I will make ₹60,000. Even if I deduct money for rent and electricity, I will still make a profit of ₹20,000 per month. Using that money, I can open another centre. I want to study law and make a profit. I have many things going on in my mind, I have many plans. I must achieve a lot in life. I don't want to remain dependent on my parents. I plan to settle in either Gurgaon or Dubai. If I live in Dubai, I'll buy a house in Dubai, then I can keep shifting between the two. I don't want to live here in Dakshinpuri. I am going to try everywhere, I'm sure I'll find success somewhere.

Shekhar works two to three jobs simultaneously. His network is so expansive that he also has the reputation of managing to get jobs for his friends. Does his education give him the confidence to dream and plan for his life?

His entrepreneurial skills and a clear sense of ambition in life seem to challenge what the state failed to give him—a house, security and good education—and what he is now determined to acquire in his life.

While Shekhar is able to find employment through his network of friends, we recall that Alok broke down while sharing his struggles to find employment. There was a deep resentment towards the government for failing to provide employment opportunities, which clearly reflected in his quivering voice and controlled tears during the interview:

> It is the government's responsibility to provide jobs. If we have passed out from a government school or university, it is the responsibility of the government to provide us jobs according to our interest and knowledge. Additionally, in today's time, MNCs are coming to set up business here and they come with their own set of employees. Therefore, we can't get jobs there either.

> We also have certain shortcomings. For example, we learn basic computer skills for six months but then don't follow it up with the advanced course. Then we step out in the job market only to realize how advanced everything has become; nobody wants to hire unless they know how to do coding. So, I'm thinking now that I'll learn Tally (a computer data entry skill); my chances of a job will increase then.

Alok has had a difficult time during his school days where he had to take up several jobs to support his education. He tells us,

I was working in an office in CP that did tiffin service. My job was to distribute tiffins. I would leave my house at 8 in the morning. Till 10 I would finish packing and assembling the tiffins, and then carry the heavy load on my back up to 20 floors. I was paid ₹5000 for this. I worked there for two years till I completed my Class 12. Many boys leave school in Class 11, but I was determined to complete my schooling. The money for my books and coaching came from there. I also paid for Surajchand's (younger brother) education. I have never wasted my parents' money. I learnt Java coding from a government institute so that I don't have to pay ₹1000 at a private coaching centre.

He shared in his interview the sense of responsibility he has for his family and his younger siblings. He has four brothers and one sister. All the boys went to government schools but the brother immediately older than him dropped out of school because he did not want to study.

He now works as a helper with a local DJ (who plays music at weddings). The eldest is employed in a private company as a salesman and another works as a private bus conductor. Since the two brothers are earning they decided to send their sister, who is currently in Class 5, to a private school so that she receives the education that they had all once wanted. His mother is a housewife, 'We don't even allow her to get milk from outside, we do all the outside chores for her.'

These young girls and boys, despite their struggle for decent employment, believe that education is the one resource that might enable them to fulfil their aspirations.

Rohini is enrolled in a training programme to become a police officer, while simultaneously working at a tourism office as a data operator and pursuing her BA with an open university.

She lives with her older brother, mother, and paternal aunt. She has a boyfriend whom she has been dating for a year and a half now; no one in her family knows about this. The boyfriend is studying Engineering and lives in Devli. Rohini is opinionated, very articulate, and almost fearless while speaking her mind and questioning others around her.

While she had to transfer from a private school to a government one after Class 5 due to financial constraints, her older brother continued to study in private school till he completed schooling. She explains,

I have been working since I was in Class 9. I used to tutor children studying in nursery to take care of my expenses. My mother would pressurize my brother to get a job to support the family, but he never did. So, I began working; when a mother weeps it hurts her daughter the most. I had to enrol for tuitions myself for two subjects when I was in Class 12. I could not focus on my studies well because of this and ended up scoring only 60 per cent in Class 12. I couldn't get admission anywhere.

Now I am studying at the Open University and financially supporting my family. I am happy. Earlier I was upset that I would not be able to attend regular college. My brother also did not want me to attend regular college because he felt it was not a serious place for study.

These discussions helped us put forth an argument for a different imagination of citizenship drawing from Snell-Rood's conception of 'getting ahead' as 'moral citizenship'. Her work with women in the Ghazipuram slums focused on how the women were able to make their lives meaningful in the city following the demolition of their settlement. She explains moral citizenship as going beyond what the state can, but fails to, provide:

> ...residents offered a type of citizenship that was not dependent on others' recognition alone, be it of government, patrons, or employers.... As residents defined their contribution to the society and sometimes rejected political society, they elaborated citizenship as an ethical concept enacted through their daily practices of work, family, and urban life. (Snell-Rood, 2015, p. 137)

Education, like moral citizenship, is a way to not give up claims to citizenship. The young girls and boys who were part of our research, while being aware of the political apathy and their own marginalization, refute the failures of the political society. Instead of giving up, they make sure to upgrade their skills, whether through English-speaking courses or computer training, in addition to attending schools and colleges, to be able to reach the job market.

While there is economic and social marginalization (based on their caste for example), education gives them the opportunity to access the public space, imagine their lives differently and also work accordingly to realize those dreams. After all, the current government has come to power through promises of 'development' that entails employment for all, among other infrastructural developments like roads and houses for all.

The vignettes above demonstrate how despite being marginalized and rendered invisible by the government and being rooted in the discourse on vulnerability, these young girls and boys also constitute the 'aspirational citizen-subject' of the political parties; they are thus part of their vote banks and of their 'imagination' of development.

Priya studies in Class 9 and lives in Dakshinpuri with her parents and sisters. She shares,

My father says that I should be independent so that I don't have to borrow from anyone. Like how we live today, we borrow from others, you won't have to live like that. My mother also says that the kind of days she has experienced, I shouldn't have to. Stand on your feet so that you can live life the way you want to. I don't want to live here. I want to be in the tourism industry. There was a lecture on it in our school the other day. I want to travel to America.

Meanwhile Aarti wants to be a fashion designer so that she can earn a good salary and live in Mumbai, 'I watch on the internet and TV what the celebrities wear. I want to make clothes for them like Manish Malhotra does.'

Anita wants a government job, like her father who works in a Kendriya Vidyalaya, 'But before I start working I want to do everything, I want to have fun, have parties, go to malls, and learn dance-music. I want to become a lawyer also. Studies mean a lot to me.'

Nazrana wants to become a nurse, 'I'll live on my own and live happily in my salary.'

CONCLUSION

The discussions on 'Education' and 'Work' helped us understand how these impact the identity and aspirations of the youth. As in every other theme explored in our research, the dynamics and deep multiple conditioning of caste, class and gender impact the lived realities of the young boys and girls living in these localities. They are fuelled by the life and times of the city they live in with the highly urbanized localities that surround their localities, access to social media and Bollywood, and the need to escape their own challenges. It was against such a background that we probed the meaning of education and employment and the trajectories these take.

In the narratives of the respondents, education is a way out of their current reality; it is a way out of poverty so that their social status improves and the girls also have better marriage prospects. Most of their parents have either never been to school or have completed schooling till secondary levels. Their parents realize the role education can play in the children's upward social and class mobility. Hence, sending children to school, especially to private schools as these are considered better equipped at imparting quality education, even at the cost of compromising their finances, is a choice many parents living here have made.

Following our interactions, we had a number of questions in the contemporary context of Skill India and Digital India, which emphasize skill building through the constant use of technology, or the use of plastic money or online banking methods like Paytm, or 'Digital Literacy' where technology would replace teachers. Who are these programmes targeting? Or who is being left behind, perhaps yet again? The government might advertise its concerns for the development of its marginalized population but the reality questions this claim.

Prakash and Alok's frustrations with being unemployed, even after completing graduation, reiterates this gap. The same gap exists also in a consumer-driven culture: one's material possessions signal one's status in society. Wants are constantly pushed to increase desire, and this, in turn, increases the already existing disparity between the state and its citizens.

This lack of employment created by the failures of the government to even imagine this cohort as citizens who have rights, has led to a gap in the aspirations of the youth living in the two localities of Dakshinpuri and Sanjay Park and the realities of their marginalization, thereby exacerbating their sense of 'impoverishment'—'a dynamic process of public decision-making in which it is considered just, right and fair that some people may become or stay poor.' (Baxi, 1988)

3

Love and Friendship
Necessity Not Indulgence

> *If we feel something is wrong, we can break up with our boyfriend/girlfriend.*
> *Friends support us in such situations and we are able to handle it* .... *Since there is no attachment left with friends after marriage, even when something is wrong, we accept our situation because no one supports us.*
>
> Nazrana, 16 years

Human beings everywhere form various kinds of relationships based on kinship, love, intimacy, care, money, labour, power, and so on. Relationships that are tied through blood or marriage are secured by rules of property and the political system. The legal and social sanction for such relationships define the 'family' as a primary group of connections, a group whose members are expected to maintain emotional ties with one another.

But with the ever-expanding onslaught of globalization on societies, the fabric of relationships is changing. Who can relate to whom is no longer restricted to traditional kinship alone. There is an entire terrain of the social, including the virtual, that allows space and opportunities to make other choices when it comes to relationships. This plays a significant role in young people's lives. Like adults who give significance to their familial relationships and those forged through work or within neighbour-hoods, young people's lives too are caught up in a network of key relationships such as those of siblings, friends, partners, class-mates, or even extended acquaintanceships such as friends of friends, and they are profoundly influenced by each one of them.

Recognizing the importance and impact of these relationships in their lives, we introduced the themes of friendship, love and marriage in our discussions with the young people of the two localities to understand and explore how young people (both girls and boys) of Dakshinpuri and Sanjay Camp experience personal relationships and what meanings such relationships hold for them. Some of the questions we had in mind were: how are these relationships influenced by differences in class and gender? In what ways do they perceive and differentiate between romantic relationships and friendships? How does access to social media affect this terrain of friendships?

Gender and Friendships

The impact of gender on friendships is an important element and has been the focus of other substantial researches as well. It is often believed that men and women relate to friendships differently; women are more emotionally intimate in their friend-ships, whereas men are less interested in disclosing their feelings to others. Being aware that there is a risk of trying to understand all experiences of friendships by way of 'general' questions on friendships and then generalising them further based on gender, we chose to talk about 'specific' friendships for a more nuanced understanding of these relationships.

Friendships: As Experienced by the Girls

It was evident to us very soon that the burgeoning and maintaining of friendship among girls revolved around their shared experience of surveillance and restrictions. Girls' friendships are based on solidarity and they usually find emotional dependence in their same-sex friendships. We call it solidarity because of the shared similarity as expressed by all the female participants in the research in experiencing the brunt of surveillance on a daily basis. In such circumstances, close friends can become saviours.

Zoya's story

'If a friend wants to go to a party and her parents are strict, we go to her place, talk to her parents and lie to them that she will be at our place,' says Zoya who has been living in Sanjay Camp since its inception. She is Muslim, lives with her mother, older brother, sister-in- law and their children; all her elder sisters are married. She is the youngest and most educated amongst her siblings. In all her sharings, she talks of how her family is very conservative and her mobility is restricted, 'In our homes it is not allowed for girls to go out; I am the only one who has studied till 1st year of college. My sisters studied only till Class 4 or 5, post which they were forced to leave school and after some time they were married.'

She has always challenged the impositions by her brother. When her brother did not allow her to get admission in college, she took money from her mother secretly, sought admission on her own and started going to college. At the same time she also started working with a local NGO as a volunteer; she is currently a full-time employee. After she became gainfully employed, her status in the family changed as she started helping her brother financially. As she shared in her interview, 'Now since I am earning, my brother asks me before buying anything or doing anything for the house.'

We will continue to explore the issue of mobility in a later section on violence and masculinity. Here we see how, through friendships, girls collectively challenge the notions of safety that confine their mobility and seek pleasure in that small window they have created through various ways of negotiation.

Girls who go out to work or study have a higher degree of access to the public space as compared to girls who drop out of school. Thus, education provides both reason and opportunity to extend their mobility and build a network, a support system in the form of friendships.

As shared by Zoya, 'We all go to the park and play there in the evening. On Sundays, we just book a cab and go to Sarojini Nagar market for shopping. After tuition, we used to go to Madangiri market just to roam around. We would be scolded every day for coming home late after tuition.'

Living in a family where opportunities of education and employment are carefully monitored, for Zoya, having close friends is very significant. She sees their role in her life as being completely different from that of her family members, 'My friends are my life. I roam around with them. We share all our problems with each other. We share everything, and no one gets annoyed by anything. I play with them and also entertain them. Families are very different. What we do with our friends we cannot do with family. We cannot enjoy with our mothers the way we can do with our friends. Friends are very caring.'

Talking to friends or chatting on the phone is the most important activity among friends. For Zoya too, chatting on

WhatsApp is one of the ways in which she maintains her friendships, and since she cannot meet her friends every day, having a phone and a social media profile becomes imperative for her. As she shared in her interview, 'My phone is my life. I cannot live without my phone for even two minutes. Once my internet stopped working for two minutes and I felt I was widowed!' Since she is not allowed to be on social media or upload pictures, we asked how she hides her friendships at home. She shared, 'I chat on my phone and nobody understands what I am doing because I am the only literate person at home. They don't know what WhatsApp is. My friends don't call me when I am at home because they know that I don't talk when I am at home.'

Komal's Story

Contrary to Zoya who is very vocal and always takes action against boys who misbehave with her on the streets, Komal is quiet and has internalized the norms of what it means to be a 'good girl', norms that have been a central aspect of every girl's upbringing. Her upbringing, like that of the others, but more stringently so, has been one of strict surveillance, especially on her mobility. She has lived with her maternal grandparents and uncle since her childhood after her parents died in an accident. Her grandmother accompanies her almost everywhere and does not leave her alone. As Komal says it,

My tuition is in the next lane, even then my Nani (maternal grandmother) drops me and picks me up. Friendship with boys is a far cry for me. I am not even permitted to talk to my cousin brothers at home. I am afraid of boys. I do not talk to any boy even if he takes the initiative, I don't respond to them. I don't know how boys behave, how they talk, what language they use...they are very different from girls.

When we asked what friendship meant to her she responded with dismay,

> Friendship is a very significant relationship. Friends help us in our difficult times when all relatives might leave us. But I never made any close friend. I have friends, but they are not like that special friend, the 'pakka' friend. All are equal for me. No one understands me. Everyone is busy in their lives, nobody cares to even listen or talk to me, and they only talk about themselves. I don't have friends in my lane, I don't talk to anyone. No one knows me in my lane; no one knows my name even.

She has internalized this fear and anxiety of going to public places and interacting with people, partially due to the terror of disappointing her grandmother and uncle,

> Since childhood, my Nani always told me to not to go out, so I never got into that habit.... Other girls roam around easily even at 10 in the night. But I'm scared of going out. I have never seen the nearby shops as I never go out to buy anything.... My mama always threatens me that I shouldn't be seen out unless I am going to computer class.

Protection of one's 'izzat' or honour is the dominant discourse that is used by her Nani to curtail her mobility. This in turn limits her contact with her friends and also prevents her from interacting with other people. She has a deep fear of women who live in her neighbourhood, since they maintain strict vigilance of every girl who lives there and then, in turn, participate in spreading rumours about them to defame the girls publicly. Gunnarson's (2015: p.108) insights on this aspect become especially relevant here.

If women are to be able to take the risk of being left unloved by men, they need to direct more of their love and support toward one another, so as to build up their reservoirs of worthiness as persons relatively independent of men's love.

Sharing personal narratives of struggles and finding solace in knowing that one is not alone in that struggle, sharing anger and laughter with each other and providing the unflinching support that perhaps one's family failed to offer—all of this shapes the moments of intimacy within female friendships here.

Friendships: As Experienced by the Boys

When we conducted the FGDs with the boys' group on questions of friendship and love, we noted that some boys were emotionally intimate in their male friendships while others were not.

Is it because they fear being vulnerable in male friendships but yearn for that safety in romantic relationships? What is the role of masculinity here? Or is our own understanding of intimacy biased because we imagined it in a way that can be conceptualized as conventionally 'feminine'?

There is an alternative way of understanding this as is explained by Migliaccio (2009), 'male intimacy that men experience is called "closeness in doing", which entails feeling close through shared activity, not through self-disclosure' (p. 229). However, we did observe that while for some boys, being expressive in their friendships was very significant, it wasn't so for others. This was exemplified in a confrontation during the group discussion on friendship within the boys' group. Four of our participants are very close friends and study in the same school. While talking about intimacy in close friendships, one of these four participants, Aman said, 'I don't share my personal things with anybody, not even with friends.'

Immediately, Anil furiously reacted, 'Friends who don't share are two-faced (*dogle*).'

His other friends too got offended by the original comment. They reacted by saying, 'Now let's see where you go to cry when you break up with your next girlfriend.'

Generally, the idea of fun or pleasure is always associated with male friendships, because boys and men are able to access public spaces more to hang out with their friends as compared to the number of girls and women who can do the same. Having fun in the public space is still a distant dream for girls and women as their presence outside of the private space is constantly questioned. Nonetheless, the global market has created a landscape of 'protected fun' for middle- or upper-class women which is related to ideas of consumption and safety and it is made possible via spaces such as malls or night clubs. This consumption-driven pleasure is, however, not accessible to working-class women, as most of them do not have the means to 'buy' these spaces as 'commodities'.

Who really can have fun then? This is a question asked by many including Shilpa Phadke, Sameera Khan and Shilpa Ranade (2011) in their pathbreaking study *Why Loiter?* that focuses on women and public spaces in Mumbai.

For the purposes of our research too, following on from what we have discussed above, fun or pleasure, which is associated with consumption, was well reflected in the narratives of the boys we spoke to, and this aspect is explored further in the chapter on masculinity later. It can be said here though that in the context of our male participants, 'hegemonic masculinity'[1] could be defined as having a girlfriend, having a fair complexion, belonging to the upper caste, being employed at an office (doing work that involves the use of computers), owning branded mobile phones, wearing fancy clothes bought from malls, partying in clubs with friends and travelling in cars.

It must also be stated that the idea of friendship for boys is a conflicting one and is different from that for girls. Having a lower degree of restriction on their mobility, the boys' friendships reflect different interpretations of solidarity. For some, for instance, emotional support required at the time of break-ups in romantic relationships creates male bonding.

Prakash and Aman became close friends after Aman broke up with his girlfriend. Until then they were just acquaintances. During Aman's interview, he said, 'I had a girlfriend, and after we broke up I was very upset and felt suicidal. I confined myself inside my house and did not talk to anyone. But Prakash *bhai* supported me a lot. He used to come every day and talk to me. He made me realize that life is beyond this and made me feel better.'

For many of the boys, solidarity revolves around the pressures and expectations of patriarchy—to be a financially independent man who will be able to support the needs of his family. Hence, being part of networks that will allow them to get jobs and money in times of need is one of the core reasons for maintaining friendships.

The fact that boys' friendships revolve around being there for each other in times of monetary requirement, to help with employment and for having networks for safety within

---

[1] Rosalind Gill (2007) in her book 'Gender and Media', talks about hegemonic masculinity within masculinity that recognizes multiple masculinities, some more powerful than the others.

Dakshinpuri and Sanjay Camp (they shared that they accompany each other post 9 pm because of the unsafe environment at night), reflects on how deeply patriarchy has structured their ideas and roles within friendships. In effect, the burden of financial responsibilities becomes the very basis of male friendships here.

Prakash, who is among the older participants in our research, has a network of friends who are his source of information. He shares with us that he finds meaning in friendship through the sharing of knowledge and support. He belongs to the Barua community of Rajasthan. He lives with his mother, father and an elder brother and they have been living here since the inception of Dakshinpuri. He has completed his graduation but is unable to find employment. He was deeply stressed and demotivated during his second interview with us, as he shared, 'Getting a job is very difficult nowadays. I learnt everything, did various courses such as basic computers, mobile repairing, stenography but nothing is happening. I have lost all hope in myself, lost all self-motivation.'

Prakash wanted to become a teacher, specifically a computer-skills teacher, so that he could share his knowledge and learning with others. He is however aware that he cannot achieve this goal because he does not know how to apply for such jobs. This was a common narrative among our participants; they had aspirations but did not have access to the required information to realize these aspirations. We observed during our discussions with him that Prakash's friendships revolve around this particular need. He told us,

> I ask my friends, those who are working. They have told me about the forms that are supposed to be filled. To get a job in the private sector we need a reference from some senior

person. In the government sector we have to compete. We sit together in the evenings in an open area near our house. We ask each other what each one is doing, are they employed or not. Some people are unemployed and those who are employed, we ask them to inform us about vacancies. We only talk about this now.

Aman's Story: Friendship and Aspirations

Aman belongs to a Hindu family and has recently given his Class 12 examinations but he failed in one of the papers. His father shifted to Delhi from Bihar long ago in search of a job. He lives with his mother, father and three sisters; he tells us that he experiences his friendships through his aspirations.

During our fieldwork, Aman started working with a call centre in Dakshinpuri which he later left due to disagreements over his remuneration. The change reflected in his way of talking or the way he dressed from our initial phase of fieldwork to the time he got his first job at the call centre was stark. He would show off his debit/credit cards during the interview; once he reflected, 'Now I talk less; my family is also seeing the changes. Some people think that I am egoistic now.'

When we talked to him about his friendships, he responded,

I have only one friend in Dakshinpuri. All my friends are outside of Dakshinpuri. I have friends in CP, Janakpuri and Ghaziabad...we spend most of our time outside Dakshinpuri; we go to Ansal Plaza or to the malls. Earlier we used to go in autos wearing weird clothes; we didn't know anything back then! But now my friends have a car and we go in that. We dress up in a way that suggests we do not belong to this area. My girlfriend added me to her friend's WhatsApp group.

We all met one day and became friends... my other friends are from Facebook. I have 5000 friends on Facebook out of which I have met 500.

Aman continuously tried to distance himself from his caste and his place of living either through the kind of clothes he chose to wear or the friends he made. He described his friendships in accordance with his class aspirations, with people who drive cars, go to clubs, have big houses and shop only at malls, perhaps in the hope that through these friendships he would be able to belong to the class he aspires to, paving the way for upward class mobility.

Homosexual Love

When we asked the boys' group whether romantic relationships can happen between same-sex people, they gave a wide range of responses. To quote some:

They are called 'kinnar', I have seen it on TV.

It is a bad thing, never do it.

Such things are done between girls not between boys.

Your family will not increase and also law doesn't permit it.

Love can happen but not marriage as the family will never accept it.

It is their experience and their choice we can't say anything.

The kind of violence that happens with girls is because of this only, they should not bring their love in public.

They shared an instance of a lesbian couple who got married and were staying in Dakshinpuri itself. But later, they were forced to move out of this place.

Cross-sex Friendships

In Dakshinpuri and Sanjay Camp, opportunities for friendships with people of the opposite sex are restricted and come under heavy surveillance. Despite this, they are able to form and maintain cross-sex friendships. We have used the latter term after Alan Booth and Elaine Hess's 1974 article entitled 'Cross-sex Friendships'.

As one sees in similar studies in other parts of the world,[2] here as well, our young participants had all made friends within their own environment—either in their schools, tuition centres or through their involvement in the NGO working in the area. Schools provided them with a space wherein they formed same-sex friendships with people who lived in or close to Dakshinpuri and Sanjay Camp. They can move around without inhibitions with these friends in the public space within these two areas. They express their friendship by holding hands, hugging each other and hanging out at parks and eating joints. Unlike schools though, tuition centres and the local NGO-run centre provide spaces where participants have the opportunity to establish 'cross-sex' interactions as well and have intimate relationships with people living in their neighbourhood, something that is otherwise prohibited in the community.

Siddharth shared with us in this regard,' Only when I come to the NGO centre, do I talk to girls, otherwise it is not allowed. People stare when you talk to girls in our area.'

---

[2] In the study by Wellman, Carrington and Hall (1988) with people living in East York (a suburb of Toronto), it was found that, ' an overwhelming majority of personal relationships were formed within a few well-defined contexts, such as school, work or neighbourhoods and few relationships were formed outside these contexts' (p. 400).

The socialization process during one's childhood through the institutions of families, communities and schools, directly or indirectly segregate activities and behaviours for girls and boys. Girls are encouraged to be submissive and take responsibilities of the household, which is also reflected in the kinds of games they play and the kind of toys they are given.

In Dakshinpuri and Sanjay Camp, these processes of socialization happen in a more controlled environment for girls, especially after they attain puberty, making the possibility of cross-sex friendships/interactions far lower for them. Yet it does not stop them from making friends with boys, and finding safe spaces that allow them to converse comfortably protected from the public gaze.[3] The consequences of being caught include stricter control of the girl's mobility to the point that she may even have to stop going to school; the boy, however, could escape with just a firm warning.

Tara, a 16-year-old participant who has been living in Sanjay Camp since her childhood and has always been awed by the restrictions imposed on the girls in the locality, says, 'We are not allowed to talk to people in our lane, not even to a fellow girl; talking to boys is beyond our imagination.'

Spaces for Romantic Relationships

There are various places in and near Dakshinpuri that are called 'love areas' where couples find space to spend their intimate time,

[3] Kabita Chakraborty (2015), in a study conducted on the mobile phone culture among the youth in the urban slums of Kolkata, describes a roof of a local home as a 'unique space, which was private and secure, it allowed young people to gather in relative safety to perform multiple desires and identities that are considered to be risky in the slums; for example they were able to try on revealing clothes, dance in mixed-sex groups, and develop relationships' (p.197).

such as Welcome Restaurant, the local park, a narrow lane between the rear walls of houses, on the slope leading to a temple and behind the neighbourhood bank.

Among these, Welcome Restaurant which is located in nearby Madangiri Market is very significant in everybody's narrative. This space allows the young people to safely interact with each other as it has a basement which protects them from prying public eyes. Interestingly, as we found during the research, there are boys, as well, who have been affected by the restrictions and surveillance around cross-sex friendships.

Varun shared his deep-seated fear of talking to girls,

I can talk to the girls here now. But earlier I just could not. If I need to ask something, then I approach them. There are a few boys who are scared of girls. Most girls are able to talk to boys, but there are some who cannot. I feel very scared inside. What if someone says something to me? I can talk to only those girls who live nearby. I have never had a friend who is a girl. I can't talk to the girls who come here like everyone else can. I don't know how to talk to a girl. I won't even approach a girl if she's just standing there alone! I don't come here on my own when you call us. What if someone stops me and asks me where I am going? Or the girls who come here on the 1st floor, if they stop me and question me? I've thought of a reply as well, I'll tell them that I have come here to attend a meeting. But if I'm crossing by this centre, I won't ever come up on my own.

Identity and Friendships

Friendships in contemporary societies are understood to be relationships that are voluntary, and their establishment is very much a matter of personal preference. Friendships are the relationships through which identity is shaped and built. Development theories see adolescent friendships as an important framework for identity formation. Through this perspective, young people choose their friends either on the basis of similarities to conform to their own aspects of identity or to adopt new aspects of the other's identities which they find lacking in themselves. This is easier for some than for others.

Rohini and Zoya

Rohini and Zoya became friends when they both started volunteering at the NGO. They both had different personalities as described by Rohini in her interview,

> I met Zoya here. Initially I didn't like her because of her language and the way she talks. She is very outspoken and uses abusive words to give back to boys on the streets in front of everyone. But later, I started liking her and we became good friends. Slowly I also learnt her language and now I enjoy it although I still can't use it publicly the way she does.

Rohini is able to adapt to new things so that she can participate in her friendships—it's a good example of changing one's own identity for a friend.

Komal and Priya

It is difficult for Komal to adapt to different friends because of her restricted upbringing. Priya is Komal's closest friend and they both go to school, and attend tuition classes and computer classes together. Komal remarked during our discussion,

Priya always asks me to go with her to the market, etc., but I always refuse as I am not allowed to go out unless it is for tuitions. She always responds to all the comments that boys make on the street. I try to shut her mouth; I am very scared of boys. She keeps asking me—did I see this, did I see that. But I just look down at the ground and keep walking. She gets angry with me also for being so docile.

Here, Priya is helping Komal in breaking away from her own fears and building her identity differently, but Komal remains uneasy when it comes to accepting these changes.

For some of the young people we spoke to, especially the boys, friendships are about aspirations, about befriending those who are living a better life in more affluent locations of Delhi—the world outside Dakshinpuri. For a while it makes them different people, one can even say that it 'changes' their identity.

Shekhar shares with us, 'I have good friends who live in flats and go to clubs... the agenda of my life is to keep making friends. Someone or the other will help me in my hour of need.'

Friendships on Facebook also play a significant role in shaping young people's identity as Facebook allows users to 'create' their profile and interact with others in keeping with the profile they have curated for themselves. Carefully selecting the photographs and videos one uploads is thus motivated by the desire to make a favourable impression on one's friends and others who might have the potential to become friends. The criterion for choosing a profile picture is to look 'good' in it and there are numerous easily available apps with features for enhancing a picture to achieve the desired effect—making the colour tone of one's face lighter, adding a pink hue to the cheeks, redness to the lips, and so on Naturally, in many ways this ends up reproducing/reiterating popular cultural gender stereotypes.

The group concurs on this point. 'Personality changes because of Facebook. I check out how other people put pictures, how they chat and try to do things differently,' says Aman. Surajchand's adds, 'It creates a different identity when friends like or comment on my picture.'

With increased access to smart phones, the Internet and social media platforms like WhatsApp and Facebook, young people are finding ways to negotiate these boundaries of surveillance and desire. Having a mobile phone allows them to communicate with their friends and boyfriends/girlfriends at any time of the day or night. For some girls, a phone gives them the anonymity that allows them to be in multiple relationships simultaneously.

> *'I have had many boyfriends. I would talk to them over phone but never meet them.'*

In fact, we found that social media has served as an extremely productive channel for girls to engage with their desires while maintaining secrecy. WhatsApp has allowed them to make friends with people who live in distant places like Gurgaon and Mumbai. Sharing of numbers within their circle of friends leads to a wider circulation of information and new friendships are thus born.

Interestingly, both groups shared the fear of approaching, or taking the initiative to talk to, the person of the opposite sex. Although there is a lack of safe spaces within the community to interact with each other without being seen, both boys and girls desire to have such opportunities, as was reflected even in the group discussion on the theme of education. When we asked the participants to imagine a school of their own, almost all of them, except two, spoke of a co-ed school.

The Hesitation about 'Love'

When we conducted the FGDs around friendship and love, we noted that none of the youth used the word 'love' directly; they had different terms to identify romantic relationships such as 'someone special', 'main love' or 'that kind of friendship' (*wo wali dosti*).

There was a lot of hesitation and inhibitions in talking about love which manifested itself in giggling and occasional blushing when we used the word 'love'. Suddenly, they also became very cautious about our audio recording and one of the boys asked us in a very low-pitched voice 'Will you share all of this with other people?'

The reluctance among boys and girls in using the word love illustrates how the phenomenon appears to be socially unacceptable. In turn, this creates a different aura around the experience of love which is considered not to be a banal experience and thereby sets it apart from its own everydayness.

Fear of Girls in Approaching Boys

In one of the FGDs on the theme of love, girls shared that they cannot propose to boys. We asked why and their responses were:

Girls never say that they love anyone, they show it through various gestures—smiling, blushing....

If a girl takes the initiative she will be considered characterless and they will say she can do this with any boy... boys can randomly propose to anyone on the street…and then they spread the news among their friends….

If we propose and later we break up they blame us that 'you were the one who was running behind me'. We are scared of such allegations… for us our 'izzat' is more important.

'Love is not wrong but when we talk about it to someone it feels like something is erroneous. The word love is not incorrect but the thinking about it is wrong,' says Prakash during a discussion. Talking about love was a bit difficult for Prakash; he had inhibitions about it initially. When we asked about his opinion he would always respond by saying, 'Other people are more experienced than me on this topic, you ask them not me.'

Raj, like other male participants, expressed the difference between friendship and romantic relationships by saying,

We can be frank with friends in public spaces; we can shout with them so that people understand that we are friends. There is no hesitation with friends. But we can't hang out with our lover in nearby places because of the fear of parents and neighbours. With lovers, we are a little scared if she feels bad and we also remain afraid that she can leave us any time. We don't care about friends when we have a girlfriend…. What we can do with our lover we cannot do with our friends.

When we asked him to spell out what he can do with a lover which he cannot with his friends, he replied, 'I will tell you if you don't feel bad. We can't kiss or smooch our friends, but we can do that with our lover.'

The mention of physical intimacy in a romantic relationship was made only by him among all the participants, although when he did say it, the other boys agreed blushingly. This was completely missing from the girls' narratives.

Even though there was hesitation in talking to us about love and closeness with a partner, it became evident very soon that boys and girls have different ideas of love, ideas which had clear underpinnings in Bollywood. When we asked Prakash to talk about his favourite romantic movie, he said, 'I like the movie *Mohabbatein* because that movie tells us that we should love the heart and soul of the person and not just the body. Most movies show that we should not love someone based on their looks but love them for their heart.' But contrary to his fantasies of how love ought to be, when he saw a couple nearby, he was shocked about how a boy appearing to be from a 'low' area could be holding hands with a fair girl. 'Love is blind maybe,' he then remarked.

We also asked the girls to talk about their favourite romantic movie and their ideas of love. The responses covered a wide range:

Love never sees the looks of the person, love can happen with anyone even if the girl is fat and has dark complexion because love is blind.

Even if the boy fights with the girl there should be understanding between them.

People can do anything for love, they can die for their love and can even leave their parents.

He doesn't touch the girl without her permission and respects her.

Some of the girls shared their attraction towards the physical appearance of popular film 'heroes': 'I like the lips and eyes of Zineth Sheik; he is very attractive, and I fantasize a lot about him'; 'I like the face and body of Tiger Shroff.' One of the girls shared that she likes the story of a video song which shows the relationship of a married couple in which the girl loves the boy a lot, but the boy behaves badly with her and ignores her: 'This song shows that girls cannot leave their husbands even if they don't love them and even if the husbands behave badly. But boys can leave us whenever, (why) because girls are emotional.'

When we asked the girls how they imagine their love, they shared a list of restrictions that they expect that their 'someone special' would liberate them from:

He would allow them to study further and work outside.

To be with their friends and not doubt them even if they have male friendships.

He should be open minded.

He would cook for them and accept them as they are, and most importantly, would not be violent with them.

Therefore, the girl's aspirations and expectations from love is an experience of 'being loved', which is largely based on the experience of being treated better than one could demand or expect (Gunnarsson, 2015, p. 108). While the girls imagine their love to bring freedom and better status as a person for them, the expectations that boys have from love is rooted in their identity as controllers and (up)holders of patriarchal values. Their hope is that their partners would not only abide by those norms but also strengthen them.

When we asked the boys how they imagine their love, their belief represented the cultural gender stereotypical expectations that are encouraged in women, such as:

Should have fair complexion
Be good mannered and soft in her dealings
Be cultured (*sanskari*)
Be respectful to her elders (his parents, etc.)
Be caring towards her husband
Wear clothes that would not offend others (cover her body
   and wear what society approves of)

Their responses were evidently in keeping with what is considered the 'normative ideals of femininity' which make women desirable.

CONCLUSION

Ideas of love and friendship and the critical role social media plays in this, is one aspect of young people's lives in resettlement colonies that we have tried to understand in this chapter. As is clear from the discussion above, there is neither a simple definition of love or friendship that emerges nor a homogenous experience of it. Yet, we are conditioned to compartmentalize the definitions almost as if the experiences that they enable can be segregated from one another.

From the idea that love is eternal to establishing that there is one and only one true love (*sachha pyaar*), to how love entails a performance of the normative roles of femininity and masculinity—for our participants, Bollywood is unanimously and undeniably that one source of information that defined and dictated how to live and conduct one's friendships and love following a linear meaning/description of both.

It also emerged quite clearly that in Dakshinpuri and Sanjay Camp, opportunities for cross-sex friendships are restricted and kept under strict surveillance. Schools, tuition centres and participation in activities organized by the local NGO provide the only spaces where these fleeting moments of interaction, permissible yet controlled, are available to the young people. Friendships that brew here could then be continued outside in public spaces like parks and malls where they 'cannot be seen' by others who may report it to their families. The consequences of being caught include enforcing a stricter control on the mobility of girls where the latter could even be forced to drop out of school; the boy, as mentioned before, usually escapes with a firm warning. However, with increased access to smart phones, the Internet and the consumption of social media platforms like WhatsApp and Facebook, girls in these localities are finding ways to negotiate the boundaries of surveillance and desire.

Girls who are first-generation learners have ensured that their families cannot access their phones that are password-protected, while others have found apps that, in turn, hide these social media apps. Girls enjoy being in multiple romantic relationships online while simultaneously being able to maintain their anonymity. For the boys, confidentiality is not a cause of concern. But love as a basis for a relationship is still a big taboo and both boys and girls during our interactions did not use the word 'love' directly. Instead they used a whole range of terms to identify romantic relationships such as 'someone special', 'main love' or 'that kind of friendship' (*wo wali dosti*).

We explored the held idea of love through the overlapping dimensions of what Stevi Jackson (2015) in her research called the 'sociality of love'—structure, meaning, practice and subjectivity. The meaning that love holds for different people is dependent on various factors. First, there are the common-sense assumptions of ideologies of love that are reinforced, renegotiated or contested in our day-to-day interactions which are linked to the practices of love. The second factor is the specific social context we inhabit which is related to the 'economic resources, class positioning and location in social division'(ibid.: p.38), which in turn limits or expands our romantic possibilities.

Friendships are embedded in solidarity, but while for girls it is about coming together because of the shared experiences of social restrictions, for the boys, friendships are a way to enact a certain kind of shared masculinity, offer support and be part of networks within an aspirational patriarchal system.

4

Marriage
Choices Defined by Caste, Class and Religion

Our research in Dakshinpuri and Sanjay Park made evident that the imagined lover and his/her qualities extend to what the girls and boys living in resettlement colonies expect from their spouses after marriage. Their apprehensions and fears revolve around caste and class and religion. Under the garb of cultural differences, some of the narratives reflected the safeguarding of caste structures, i.e., protecting them from getting polluted, which would, in turn, collapse the social order. In order to protect these structures, both men's and women's sexuality is controlled, but controls are naturally present more stringently for women. Children born of mixed-caste marriages are generally condemned.

Ara has one male friend named Rohit about whom she talked at length in the interview. Rohit is her neighbour and belongs to the Dalit community. For Ara, 'All boys are like dogs —untrustworthy.' She doesn't like any boy who lives in her neighbourhood, but when it comes to Rohit she explains it differently.

He is very nice. He always respects me, always addresses me as 'aap'. He is not like other boys of Sanjay Camp. He is very scared of my brother, so he never appears in front of him. He does all the household chores such as washing dishes and washing clothes. He is very different. I like such people; I generally go to his place. Everyone in his family knows me. His mother always says that I should become their daughter-in-law, but we are Muslim, and they are SC.[1] It is impossible.

Ara's aspirations in love and her expectations from her lover are in accordance with the kind of boy Rohit is; someone who can help in household chores, supports her in education, allows her to work, and would not impose restrictions on the kind of clothes she would wear or friends she might want to have. Despite having a friend who fulfils these criteria of a desired boyfriend/ husband/partner, she is unable to do anything about it because of the societal prohibitions on inter-faith/inter-caste relationships and the kind of violence associated with any incidence of such unions.

Ara has been able to challenge her family in all her capacity, but when it comes to marrying outside her religion or caste, it becomes a dangerous proposition,

My family is very traditional. My grandmother has a bath if these people come and sit near her. No one even shakes hands with SC people, I cannot do anything. I cannot even share with my family that I have friendships with boys. Asking them to marry me to a Hindu boy is beyond imagination.

[1] Scheduled Caste

She also apprehensively narrated the story of her cousin who eloped with her lover but her family found them and they were brutally beaten, 'My family is very orthodox (*kattar*); they will find anyone who elopes to get married no matter where they go.'

Since a Hindu enters his caste by birth, and since marriage is the institutional machinery through which birth legitimately occurs, it is to be expected that caste distinctions in India can be maintained only through the proper regimentation of the marital through the prohibition of intermarriage. This is why, in India, relatives of the prospective mates, rather than the young persons themselves, who are the parties to the marriage contract, arranged marriages and why the preliminaries to marriage are prescribed rather than spontaneous, for the endogamous rule is enforced without interference from the romantic attraction.

(Kingsley Davis, Intermarriage in Caste Societies, 1941, p.380).

During our discussions, Prakash shared his apprehensions in marrying a girl outside of his own caste and his anxiety of maintaining the purity of one's caste and continuing one's lineage that are consistent with the rules of patriarchy. He shared, with great worry, in his interview,

If you marry a girl who is of a different caste then where will the girls from our own caste go? Where will they find a match? Because we know our culture better, we know all the rules that we follow in our caste, we would be better able to understand a person of our own caste. But if we don't know anything about the other caste, their likes and dislikes, there will be tension. My chances of love are very less; I will do arranged marriage only.

Boys view marriage as a rupture in their friendships, as they believe that friendships change after one enters marital life. They offer the following reasons for this:

> We cannot live with friends in a house the way a husband and wife live.

> After marriage, family becomes more important and there are responsibilities towards them.

> We cannot hang out the way we do it now.

While for girls too, friendships change after marriage, this happens not because of responsibilities but due to the fact that they have to change their place of residence and they cease to have access to each other's addresses or phone numbers.

According to our participants, marrying for love is more of a modern western phenomenon that upholds ideas such as individuality and individual freedom. It seems to stand inherently against the accepted Indian cultural connectedness of marriages arranged by families or others in the community.

> Love marriage doesn't stay for long. People get bored in it after a point. Also, the family is never happy with love marriage. People attend a wedding ceremony in arranged marriages and they all remain happy. The girl who comes home in a love marriage does not respect (the family). We can love anyone, but marriage only happens within our own caste.

The above was said in a group discussion of boys and appeared as the common consensus among all the participants. It clearly reflects the anxiety of interrupting socially bound relationships as if doing so could lead to some disorder in the community.

Gender, Social Structure and Marriage

For boys, family and maintaining the lineage plays a vital role in their lives. They cannot imagine any other form of family other than one which comprises their parents, their wives and their two children, specifically a boy and a girl, which according to them is a 'complete happy family' (sukhi-sampan parivaar). In order to maintain this status quo, they cannot challenge the norms of family by marrying out of their own choice.

For Aman too, like with other boys, marriage is not a choice. He cannot imagine his life without being married,

To keep my lineage going; when two families connect through marriage it helps build more relations, which in turn can be helpful; we cannot live our entire life alone; everyone needs someone with whom they can share everything which we find with our life partner.

The two ways in which the burden of patriarchy is most conspicuous in the lives of the boys we spoke to are first, to be able to financially support their families, especially post marriage, including their wives, and second, the anxiety to procreate in order to keep their family name going. The roots of these apprehensions about marrying outside of one's own caste are to be found in the conservative community structure through which sexual relationships are supposed to be circumscribed within well-defined specific groups.

It is a different story for the girls. Girls view any form of marriage as a constraint in their lives, as they narrated during our discussion. Even though being married may provide a change from their current reality, it means giving up their freedom and their aspirations for themselves.

What do we get after marriage? Sadness and restriction—nothing else. I have seen women around me, they are only busy with their kids and families, they don't have any time for themselves.... We cannot achieve our dreams after marriage. We are tied with relationships in marriage; it is better to live alone and have the freedom to do things for oneself, wear anything, eat whatever.

Komal also feels that since she has been raised by her grandparents, she is somehow a liability for them. She shared in her interview that her uncle wants to marry her off early since they cannot keep her with them for long. She has many dreams but this fear of being married off early, without her consent, is a fear that is evidently occupying her mind. She wants to be a doctor but her uncle refuses. He has given her limited time to make her decision; she is thinking of choosing the profession of a teacher as it will take less time and require less money than others to pursue and accomplish. Her grandmother has a lot of anxiety about Komal's studies. Komal shares with us about this,

Nani scolds me that I am only interested in myself because I think about becoming a teacher. In our caste, girls don't get a good match if they are too educated, since boys don't study much. One of my cousins studied engineering but now she is not getting any offers of marriage.'

Marrying outside her caste or having a love marriage is a distant dream for Komal. If anyone finds out in her family about any girl's relationship, they forcefully marry her off with someone or kill her. She sounds terrified as she says,

If any of my family members find out that I am roaming around with a boy, they will just kill me. To begin with,

I cannot even think about this as I am very scared of my family, I don't have enough courage to do this.

When the girls talked about their imagination of future lovers/husbands who will allow them to work, wear clothes of their choice, and so on, in the hope of being the person they desire, it is also with the hope of gaining the support that is missing in their present lives.

It must also be added here that the fact that their conception and fantasy of marriage has reflections of Bollywood is obvious to all, given the huge influence that Bollywood movies and their world of make-believe have on Indians of the current generation as well as previous ones. As Chakraborty (2016) states in her study, '(young women's) expectations of marriage align with popular Bollywood culture; in its ideal form, marriage is a partnership between two people who love and care for each other' (p. 427).

When we asked the girls to imagine their lives if they were unmarried and 30 years of age (to include who they would be living with, what would they be doing and how they imagine their emotional state at that time), in comparison with boys who could only imagine a possibility of marriage as a certainty and their immediate family around them, the girls were able to imagine life differently with diverse 'structures' of family like living in, being a single mother, and so on. In our discussion about this, Nazrana said, 'I will be a nurse and in a live-in relationship with my partner.' Afsana too shared, 'I will remain unmarried and adopt a child from any orphanage. I can live with any of my friends even if she is married and has a husband.'

But when the same question was posed to the boys' group, it was difficult for them to imagine a life outside the structure of one form of family. Varun said, 'I will be doing some private job and will be living with my parents; marriage will definitely happen.' Like Varun, Raj shared with us, 'I will be staying with parents and we will definitely be full of regret if we don't marry by the age of 30.'

It is our understanding that the boys were probably unable to imagine a different life because they don't feel the need for it. No restrictions are imposed upon them by their family in terms of mobility, or when it comes to decisions regarding what to wear or having a phone, and so on. They are not even looking at exploring other ways of living since there is no need for liberation from family surveillance. For the girls on the other hand, freedom from restrictions and the ability to decide what they want to do and where they want to go is a dream, an aspiration, almost a necessity.

CONCLUSION

While class and caste overshadow the reality of love and marriage for both boys and girls in Dakshinpuri and Sanjay Camp, there is a difference in how both genders form friendships and respond to marriage.

Romantic relationships are coloured by the fantasies and conflicting opinions of how girls and boys perceive prospective lovers/future spouses. There is a tension between how girls live their traditional life pre-marriage and what they feel they would be able to attain (of their aspirations) post-marriage when their husbands would (hopefully) allow them to live their lives on their terms.

Boys, on the other hand, are living out their aspirations in this regard currently with no restrictions on their mobility or their appearance or clothing. Barring economic and employment aspirations, boys do not experience or feel that something very fundamental is missing from their lives as the girls do. While girls see marriage as a way of coming out of their parents' shadow and have more agency as married women, boys see marriage as a marker of their masculine roles of bread earner of the family and protector of the honour of the family. Boys shared with us very clearly that they expect themselves and their future partner to adhere to the norms of family post-marriage and this would be non-negotiable as a quality in their future wife.

Boys were also ready to sacrifice their luxury of having unlimited time with friends and loitering in markets once they were married, and they recognized that after marriage they would have less time to be with their friends because of their familial responsibilities. This awareness of their role and some restrictions on them as married men was not expressed as a burden or unpleasant phase of their life. Their roles and responsibilities as married man, as husband, as son are accepted and internalized in as natural a process as their biological identity of being male. However, while boys did not seem to recognize the burden and expectations of patriarchy and its effects on them, girls were not only vocal about their feelings of suffocation and the lack of freedom, they were also invested in imagining an alternative reality for themselves where they could have lives outside of familial structures.

It is also interesting to note that while girls are more open to enter into inter-caste and inter-class marriages, boys see themselves as custodians of caste purity and want to uphold their caste identity for something as important as marriage. The idea of masculinity is also closely tied to the idea of a pure lineage (not polluted by inter-caste/inter-religious mingling) and purity of blood, which is ensured through caste segregation.

We also observed that despite being in an environment where boys are not strictly governed by their community norms as the families in these resettlement colonies have migrated to cities long ago, their aspiration to not breach their caste affiliations is very strong. They not only think that it is their moral responsibility to marry girls of their own caste and religion, they are also driven by their sense of masculine responsibility to protect the family and caste honour. Being custodians of family honour, they also feel obliged not to cross boundaries of caste and religion, as it would mean bringing dishonour to their fathers and in turn compromising their authority within the family if social norms defined by their caste and religion are broken.

5

Technology
A Must-Have

In the present times, our homes have been completely transformed to imbibe multimedia culture in a way where we can no
longer imagine our lives without it, be it for leisure, work, friends
or family. Rigorous advertising regularly updates us with the
possibilities of such technologies as used in e-commerce or
virtual classrooms that reflect the kind of environment we live
in. Mobile phones and social media are the most easily accessible
among the various media and communication technologies and
form an ordinary yet intrinsic feature of young people's lives. It
is worth reiterating here how during a group discussion, one of
our research participants exclaimed, 'My phone is my life. I can't
live without my phone for even two minutes. Once my internet
stopped working for two minutes and I felt I was widowed!' This
stark comparison with a lived relationship compelled us to study
the interconnections between media, youth and the state.

In this chapter, we explore the ways in which mobile phones
have changed young people's lives in Dakshinpuri and Sanjay
Camp and how they navigate terrains of friendship, mobility,

romance and leisure through social media. In what ways do girls and boys present themselves to others through online platforms? In this time when all information about government schemes or policies is shared through social media, how does this population access such information? Although there is a plethora of information and communication technology (ICT)-based devices available such as computers, tablets, mobile phones and laptops, for the purpose of this research we have focused on the use of mobile phones and social media sites/applications such as Facebook and WhatsApp.

Gender Differences in the Use of Social Media

Among our participants, except for three girls, everyone had their personal smart phones with data packs, which they use for a wide range of things such as online shopping, listening to music, watching videos, to order food and to book a cab. But they primarily use it for WhatsApp and Facebook. All our participants who had personal phones have had Facebook and WhatsApp profiles for more than a year. We found in our research that gender differences are present in the ways in which girls and boys use these social media profiles. When asked about how they use these applications, girls shared that they enabled them to be in contact with their peers, to reinforce their pre-existing relationships and, for some, to upload their pictures. Two of our participants among the girls were neither allowed to have a profile on Facebook nor use WhatsApp or upload their photographs. To negotiate these restrictions, one of them has two profiles, one with a different name to maintain anonymity.

Zoya shared that she has downloaded a software application on her phone that hides all the social media apps which is in turn password-protected. She also has a Facebook profile under a different name that allows her to chat with random people and upload her pictures, enabling her to maintain confidentiality around her identity. She uses her education too to challenge the restrictions imposed by her family, especially with her brother. As she shared,

> My brother doesn't know how the internet functions. He keeps asking me about its functionality. So I taught him the functions of YouTube on which he can play videos but didn't tell him about WhatsApp or Facebook, otherwise he will know that I am active on social media.

Rohini shared that her brother had access to her password, and thus maintains control over her mobility online. Since the mobile phone revolution is new to the older generation, most of the participants' parents use the *dabba* phone, an old-fashioned Nokia phone, restrictively, to call or receive calls. They have been taught to use these phones by their children. Although generally fathers of our young participants possess personal phones, mothers either don't have one or use the family phone, as most of them are illiterate. None of the parents use Facebook or WhatsApp.

For the boys in our research, it is a platform where they can upload their pictures to see how many likes and comments they get, thereby gauging how popular they are in their friends' circle. As shared by one of the boys, 'I want to show on FB where I go, with whom I hang out and how much fun I have.' Like the girls, some of the boys too have more than one profile to maintain anonymity, but this, they claim, is to be able to chat with random people and to 'perform their moral duty as a friend', explained further as in order to check whether their friends are being 'cheated on' by their boyfriends/girlfriends. The lack of familial restriction as far as the use of social media on phones for the boys is clear when it was shared in our discussion that they could upload their pictures however they wanted to and often kept changing their profile pictures.

While romantic relationships are generally considered socially unacceptable as discussed in Chapter 3, both girls and boys we spoke to continue to be involved in them. Having mobile phones allows them to communicate with their partners at any time. For some girls, the phone provided them the anonymity to be in a relationship without ever seeing the person involved, as shared by one of our female participants, 'I have had many boyfriends. I would talk to them on the phone but never meet them.' Even though it is expected that women abide by certain norms and maintain the 'good girl' identity all the time, 'the reality is that young women perform multiple identities at different times and in different spaces as they consciously navigate private and public domains' (Chakraborty 2016:422).

One such space is provided by social media through which girls play out their desires while maintaining secrecy. WhatsApp has allowed them to make friends with people who live in distant places like Gurgaon and Mumbai. Sharing of numbers within their friends' circle leads to a wider circulation of information and new friendships are thus born.

Like any other public space where women are one of the 'unbelongers' and 'they feel compelled to demonstrate at any given point that they have a legitimate reason to be where they are' (Phadke, Khan, & Ranade, 2011:8), social media websites have also become that space where women's presence is disturbing for others. While some of them are not allowed to access mobile phones on the pretext that it distracts them from their studies, others who are permitted to use them are constantly monitored by their brothers or fathers. 'My paternal uncle is also on FB. He follows my online activities very closely. He interrogates the people I chat with as well.'

> The mobile phone is helping parents stay in touch with their female children as they extend their schooling career... to reduce the insecurity of parents who are worried for their daughters' safety... but it has also brought another set of issues, with parents worried that girls are not misusing their freedoms and the mobile phones to develop romances.
>
> (Chakraborty 2015: p.204)

Since there are privacy issues on social media websites, most sites allow users to adjust their settings to control who can view or have access to their profile and posts. Girls, more than boys, are concerned about their privacy settings and the kind of photographs they can upload. For example, one girl is allowed to upload group photographs but not those in which she is alone. Others are not allowed to upload their pictures at all, which they explain by saying, 'I'm scared that people will misuse the photos.' Their concerns about privacy and identity disclosure on websites predisposes them to interact with individuals they either already know or it means that they must make friends very cautiously, 'We first check their accounts, the kind of photos they upload. Before accepting their friend request we ask them who they are and how they know me; for all we know it is a boy pretending to be a girl.' It is imperative that access to technology does not undermine the surveillance that they have internalized in terms of self-discipline, so that they don't inadvertently cross the *lakshman rekha* marked by their family members.

Self and Social Media

Social media websites such as Facebook allow users to 'create', even 'curate' their profile and interact with others accordingly. Carefully selecting the photographs and videos one uploads is motivated by the desire to make a favourable impression on their friends and others who might have the potential to become friends. One of our participants remarked in this regard, 'Personality changes because of Facebook. I check out how other people put pictures, how they chat and try to do things differently.' The concept of liking and commenting on the photographs plays a significant role in the way they choose to present themselves. As another participant shared, 'It creates a different identity when friends like or comment on my picture.' A picture can make them look 'good' and they can make themselves fairer and add colour to their cheeks or lips by using apps which have the requisite features to change the image in keeping with how they want to 'ideally' appear. As mentioned in Chapter 3, this does lead to the reproduction of prevalent cultural gender stereotypes.

The culture of 'likes and comments' used by social media websites can be best understood through the analytic distinction between the signifier and the signified (Gill 2007:45). For instance, Facebook allows the users to 'like' their friends' pictures/videos which they post, but this 'liking' has become an important signifier for self-approval, emotions and self-motivation, as explained by our participants in a whole range of ways:

Our feelings depend upon the likes we get.

My family always discourages me that I am not beautiful but when people comment by saying 'awesome' , 'beautiful', I feel good.

But does this create a vicious cycle of seeking validation, a competition for more 'likes' that in turn leads to jealousy among friends? The act of liking or commenting has created a structure of meaning, much like advertisements which sell products not for their use value, their functional value as objects but in terms of ourselves as social beings. Through advertising, products are given an exchange value – statements about a particular commodity are translated into statements about who we are and who we aspire to become (Gill 2007:50).

Just like owning a Rolex watch symbolizes affluence and success which is more significant than its utility, having a larger number of likes translates into validation, taking the young people closer to their aspirational selves—fair-skinned, hanging out at malls, wearing branded clothes, and so on.

During one of the focus group discussions, we gave our participants an example of a fictitious profile of a girl and a boy (respectively for the girls' and boys' groups) in which that girl/boy had uploaded a number of pictures at different places, with friends trying out different kinds of food, and so on. The overwhelming response from boys reflected the life they desired, 'If only these things happened with me too: the way he uploads pictures with girls, the way he travels, the way he can upload picture with alcohol… friendships should be done with such people who in turn have high-level friends.'

However, for the girls it was the freedom of publicly uploading pictures of themselves that was more desirable, 'Her mother must have allowed her…we don't have permission to do so; she can put a picture in which she is alone, we are only allowed to put group photographs.'

Such narrations consistently reflect the ways in which boys and girls use media differently based on how they understand their lives. Girls aspire to have an independent life where they are financially self-reliant so that they define the boundaries of their lives on their own, without the outer restrictions that the family puts on them currently. The boys on the other hand, do not have such restrictions, for example, on their mobility, hence their aspirations are also plainly different.

Access to State Services Information through Social Media

Gone are the days when people had to wait for the next day's newspaper to know about current affairs. Whether it is about the new policies introduced by the government, like demonetization or a scheme like that of the Aadhaar Card, the news quickly circulates through social media. 'We get information about LPG subsidies and demonetization through messages, advertisements and posters.' With radio shows like 'Man ki Baat', the government has entered the homes of the common person. 'On Teachers' Day, Modi was telling all of us how to prepare for our exams.'

But is the government becoming more and more distant at the same time? With demonetization leading to deaths and suicides here in Dakshinpuri and Sanjay Camp like in other parts of the country, and then the resentment following the introduction of the Goods and Services Tax, is the government really listening to the voices of the people?

During our research, since we had shared our numbers with the participants, they used to send us various messages in the form of audio or video clips through WhatsApp, which they received from unknown sources. These messages were mostly about various schemes/policies/services launched by the central government or were about issues of national concern. We decided to use a few of them to talk about state and citizenship in one of the FGDs to understand the sources of such messages and their decisions regarding which ones to forward and why.

We chose a clip showing three men dressed in skull caps, with long beards, carrying the Indian flag and shouting '*Hindustan zindabad, Pakistan murdabad, Hindustan meri jaan*'. We asked the participants to share their thoughts. Some said that they felt proud that Muslims were shouting slogans like 'Hindustaan Zindabaad'. But this led to a deeper debate about how to identify one's identity, the authenticity of such videos and their purpose. Most of the participants admitted that they barely read or viewed the messages or videos before they forwarded them. Neither did they concern themselves with cross-checking the authenticity of these forwards.

We were reminded of Rosalind Gill's view that,

(it creates) new subject position and by transforming subjectivities, it deliberately sought to detach people from their existing points of identification and to reposition them in new sets of discourse which hailed them as a 'concerned patriot', 'self-reliant taxpayer', 'clean citizen', 'digitally literate' and so on (2007).

Social media is helping us occupy new identities where subjectivities are being made and re-made in this dynamic process. Undoubtedly, 'platforms such as Facebook, WhatsApp, Instagram, Twitter seem to have emerged and are being accepted as the fifth pillar of media after print, TV, digital and radio" as per Mishra (2015).

CONCLUSION

During the personal interviews, when we asked how their lives have changed with the increased use of mobile phones, one participant shared in great detail and with nostalgia, the lost sense of 'community' he feels now with the loosening of neighbourly bonds and people becoming more individualized:

> Whenever children cry, they show them a video. No one plays with them. They get used to not doing anything physical. Whenever children do not get access to the phone they show their anger by throwing things…. We used to spend most of our time outside playing different games such as Ludo or Kanche…health was much better…. These days, people call cabs to their houses to go anywhere; earlier we used to roam here and there and had much more knowledge about places…. Distances have increased because of mobile phones and people who live far away have become more closer…. Everyone plays games on their mobile phones with strangers through the Internet, nobody sits with another person to share anything. We don't get to know about other people these days.

These feelings however are very different from the reality of the young people. Not only do they think that they cannot survive without their phones, but they also feel that the mobile phone has given them a sense of worth and the ability to engage with the outside world.

While, for boys, the phone is just as necessary and easily available as their daily needs, girls still have to negotiate hard with parents for a phone. In many instances, the girls also had a secret phone, mostly gifted to them by their lovers, which they guard with their life. Girls also face a lot of violence if parents come to know of these secret phones. Since a phone and access to various social media platforms through it is a great way for girls to interact with the outside world, parents and especially brothers of the girls maintain stringent control over these devices and their passwords. While sometimes, girls have to share their passwords with their brothers and parents, on many occasions, they are also able to manoeuvre the situation such that they have two passwords or they use apps that allow them to hide the FB and WhatsApp icons from the main phone memory screen. Sometimes, a girl will take advantage of the non-literacy of her parents and purposefully not tell them how to operate phones apart from making calls; it's a way to ensure that they don't control her activities on the phone. Almost all the girls in our research (except one) had their own Facebook pages and interacted with boys and strangers through social media.

With phones keeping young people 'occupied' at all times, they feel incomplete and at a loss without their phones. The young people we spoke to enjoy unprecedented exposure to the world outside through these phones. The access they gain into the inner circles of the world that they aspire to be part of is exciting and almost mandatory in order to feel like they are a part of the larger reality where they are not overwhelmed by the harshness of life.

On the other hand, however, there is a lack of spaces where young girls and especially young boys can talk about what they are reading, seeing and experiencing. Videos containing instances of violence are circulated regularly through You Tube. This does help in spreading awareness about such incidents, especially within Dakshinpuri and Sanjay Camp, because parents, on seeing such videos, become more cautious about the whereabouts of their children and their safety. It is difficult to assess if there is a connection between the growing incidents of violence here, the increased use of cell phones and the decreased sense of togetherness. We did get a clear sense of the use of cell phones in mobilizing support in times of conflict between groups of boys, and in spreading the news widely in order to polarize instances of conflict or violence on caste and community grounds.

6

Masculinity
A Collective Identity

When we started the research, we did not conceptualize talking or writing about masculinity. However, we soon felt that It would be ignorant of us if we continued to be oblivious to this central issue of young people's lives.

We caught a glimpse of this on the first day of the research itself when we met the boys and asked them to develop a short skit on the theme of work. The timid and petite looking boys played the roles of the women in their households and the seemingly big, boisterous ones played the fathers and husbands. There were many instances when we observed conspicuous demonstrations of masculinity, starting with how everyone looked up to the views and opinions of one boy in the group who was fondly called 'bhai'[1] by the rest of them. Keeping our observations and

---

[1] A Hindi word translated to English as older brother but has connotations of someone who has a certain level of power amongst the members of the larger group/community.

experiences in this regard in mind, we explore a few theories of understanding masculinity and its relationship with violence and education in this chapter.

First FGD on Work with the Boys

The boys performed a play in which the characters to be enacted were those of a grandfather, his son, son's wife and their two children—a school-going daughter and her college-going brother. During the play, while the brother shares stories about his girlfriend, the girl's role is limited to sharing her day at school and being told to wear a dupatta. The brother is shown escorting the sister everywhere. The grandfather shares a close bond with his grandson and spoils him with gifts like phones and bikes. The grandfather also taunts his son for being a 'lukkha', a loser, and advises his grandson to not be like his father. The wife is expressive in her desires towards her husband, occasionally pulling him into the bedroom, and obedient towards her father-in-law. Eventually the play ends with the young boy accusing his mother of having an affair with their neighbour and producing photographic evidence. The daughter sides with her mother, but the rest of the family throws her out.

The play was enacted with laughter from all the characters and members of the audience. This mix of violence and humour perplexed us, and we discussed it in the later FGDs. What decided which boy would be chosen as the female lead, would he drape a sari or carry a woman's bag—such questions reflected their struggles around masculinity. As we have already mentioned, we discussed extensively the fact that small boys were chosen to play the female leads and big, boisterous ones enacted the male leads.

Through the Eyes of Sonu: 'the Bhai of the Gali'

Sonu is 20 years old and pursuing his BA from an open university. He belongs to the Valmiki community.[2] He has a younger sister who finished her schooling last year and wants to become a teacher. Sonu proudly tells us that he will ensure that his sister becomes what she aspires to. He stays with his parents, but his mother has not spoken to any of the family members for a really long time. 'My mother is very suspicious,' he explained to us once. He admires his paternal grandfather and father for making it big in life; their family is one of the most affluent in Dakshinpuri with two cars and a bike and are known to have owned the first colour television in their *gali* (lane).

Sonu has had many girlfriends and proudly shared details of his days when he was a 'playboy', after his girlfriend got married to someone else. 'The reason why I have so many enemies here is that if I'm seen talking to a girl, her brother's friend will go snitch on me. No matter who he is in a relationship with, but his sister cannot even talk to anyone,' explains Sonu about how he has enemies here but is also revered as a the 'bhai of the gali'. His father's brother was a martyr during the Kargil War and his father is now contesting elections from Bijnor, their hometown.

Our research started with unpacking the labels that the outside world has used to describe both Sanjay Camp and Dakshinpuri—unsafe and violent. Throughout our interaction

---

[2] The Valmiki community is a caste that has historically faced exclusion and oppression in society, and members of which are frequently affected by anti-Dalit violence and repression by members of other castes. The caste draws its name from the sage Valmiki in the Hindu tradition who is traditionally ascribed with writing the epic, Ramayana.

with the boys and girls here, narratives of violence in the public domain have been plenty, and it is easy to deduce and verify from these that Dakshinpuri and Sanjay Camp are in fact violent and unsafe. The middle-class morality that dictates how spaces like Dakshinpuri and Sanjay Camp are viewed is clear from the PILs that have been filed by the middle-class citizens of the city to demolish and evacuate such settlements as they symbolize dirt, un-wantedness and unsafety (Bhan, 2016).

These spaces are then classified as 'unsafe' and 'violent' even by the state and these labels are forwarded as the justification for the gentrification of such urban spaces. The seemingly high rate of violence, then, needs to be read through a class lens and not merely taken as the obvious outcome of spatial occupancy. We have, therefore, refrained from even looking at this correlation of space and violence. What we were more interested to find out through our research was the interplay of 'masculinity' with violence in the daily lives of the boys and girls in these resettlement colonies.

The most interesting part of our study regarding masculinity became visible during the personal interviews with both the boys and girls. While the boys shared their vulnerabilities and fears about living here and about interacting with girls (specifically only during their in-depth individual interviews), the girls shared how they are learning strategies to deal with the *ched-khani*[3] that they refuse to tolerate anymore.

So, while the girls are able to understand and deal with their fears of living through some form of daily sexual harassment in the public spaces, at the same time the fears they have for

---

[3] A Hindi word used by all participants to describe unwanted sexual harassment.

the safety of their brothers in the public space are increasing. This made us think about masculinity through vulnerability and fear and not just through the performance of it as a tough, muscular man.

There are also possible interlinkages between masculinity and education. As is evident from what all our participants shared, the drop-out rate among boys is increasing while among the girls it is decreasing, with some girls even going on to college. Is there a correlation between masculinity and the increasing drop-out rate among the boys living here?

Masculinity as Socialized Norms and in Opposition to Femininity

Masculinity studies have been a separate area of research for a long time now and many theories with regard to this phenomenon have been postulated. Here, we limit ourselves to a few that best explain our scope of work.

Traditionally, men and women are expected to perform certain roles that have been prescribed to them. Friedrich Engels, in his classic work, *The Origin of the Family Private Property and the State* (1902), established the birth of patriarchy and the consequential division of roles and labour based on the sex of the person, where women are meant to be confined to the house and their sexuality needs to be controlled so that the child born only out of marriage can be declared as the rightful heir to the property taking forward the land ownership and the name of the father. The man is then expected to work outside the private domain of the household, earn money and financially provide for his family.

Once the roles have been divided, and as we observed during our research in these two resettlement colonies, it is the duty of all women and men to ensure that this order is not challenged. If and when it is challenged, there will be consequences. As we observed, however, the girls often take small but important steps to question and transgress social norms.

Afsana fights at home to ensure that she is allowed to go to school. Priya gives a befitting reply to the boys who harass her on the streets, claiming for herself the right to take risk and loiter. Zoya and Rohini become the first girls in their respective families to study in college and get jobs. Nazrana pushed the boundaries and made her father buy her personal phone.

The most direct retaliatory consequence of such transgression is that girls are forced to drop out of school, further curtailing their mobility and their experience of the outside world. Since boys must provide for their families and procreate so that their family name continues, once they have completed their education, they need to find employment otherwise they would be faced with incessant verbal taunts to mock their inability to perform their role as the breadwinner of the family.

Masculinity then is what men do in order to be counted as men, both in their own eyes and in the eyes of others. The birth of the child, with the accompanying exclamation of 'It's a boy!' or 'It's a girl!' dictates the colours s/he will wear, the toys s/he will play with, how s/he will sit, walk and talk to the more complicated experiences of emotions that s/he will be allowed to express. Our lives are contained within these normative walls of masculinity and femininity.

Masculinity studies in the West point to the two primary ways in which masculinity is experienced by boys. As Edley writes,

… there has been a steady oscillation between two basic forms of masculinity: the puritan and the playboy. The puritan consists of an austere form of masculinity, based around the values of hard work, self-discipline and religious fervour. The playboy on the other hand, is a hedonist: his life is dedicated to leisure, pleasure and general self-indulgence (2017: p.42).

In the Indian context, one of the key characteristics of being masculine extends to being able to produce a male child and contributing fruitfully to the progeny of the family, as opposed to proving manliness by showing the number of women the man can have.

It is important to place the discourse of masculinity in the context of our research participants, i.e., with young people. To continue the thread of hegemonic masculinity, the burden of patriarchy on men is seen through their sharing of how important it is for them to be able to financially provide for their families, marry a girl and provide for her and give birth to a male child who will continue their family name. And this 'ideal' of being a man is felt very strongly by boys throughout their growing-up years.

Chaitali Dasgupta in her seminal paper on understanding the phenomenon of gang violence through the formation of the ideas of masculinity during the adolescent years explains, …hegemonic masculinity not only oppresses women but also cripples relationships between men. In order to demarcate from hegemonic masculinity, workers in the field no longer apply the singular term, masculinity, but use the plural, mas-culinities, in order to find spaces for different ways that males develop their identities… age affects the formation of mascu-linities in that masculinity is accorded a different significance at differing moments during the male life cycle. (2001)

Multiple Masculinities

Participants like Shekhar and Sonu symbolized the hegemonic masculinity of Dakshinpuri and Sanjay Camp; they are big-built, and have contacts with the boys/men who are known to be local criminals. They reported engaging in physical violence themselves as well. It was interesting that both the boys framed their narratives within the caveat, 'now I have improved, and I focus on my work.'

Vishal is the playboy; he openly talks about his promiscuity and is looked upon by the others in the group as the 'experienced one'. Sandeep, effeminate in his way of walking and talking, is confident and unapologetic about his 'feminine' ways of being, like enjoying dancing and wearing a sari. The rest of the boys aspire to be the ideal masculine adult—responsible, educated and financially supportive of the family.

Masculinity is formed through power and violence. Sonu shared during the discussions about his family's reconciliation with their caste in an ambiguous way; accepting their caste in their personal lives but camouflaging it in the public:

I belong to the Valmiki caste, which as you know comes under the lower castes. Only when my father removed Valmiki from his name—he is now Rajiv Sood—was he able to get a ticket. My father knows the top politicians of Uttar Pradesh. Earlier, because of his surname, he wasn't given a ticket to contest. The top politicians do not know that we are from the Valmiki community. Because we don't look like we belong to that caste. People think we are Punjabis because of our surname. 'Sood' is Punjabi but 'Sud' is Valmiki. Everybody thinks of our caste as the lowest. Even the jobs that are reserved for us, are given to the jaat-gujjars. But now my father wants that all the votes from our community should be cast for him. There is a puja that we do where we sacrifice a pig. But we don't eat pork. We go to our village to perform the puja; not here. Here, we only eat the sweet halwa.

Sonu exemplifies the hegemonic masculinity that adolescent boys aspire to. He idealizes his father and aspires to be as brave and strong as him. He uses the connections his father has made to assert his own masculinity. Towards the latter part of the interview he reminded us that those days of him being violent and a playboy were in the past, now he has a job and is a gentleman, a 'shareef and sudhra' boy in his words.

Talking about how the boys in the neighbourhood get involved in gang violence, Sonu shared,

The boys who become involved with violence are between 14–15 years of age. The older boys hit the younger ones. The younger ones then go to these very older boys asking for work. They also get arrested in the process. You get spurious alcohol for ten rupees here; then there is betting and gaanja (weed). One boy corrupts ten more with him! But I don't feel scared to live here. See, my paternal uncle, who lives in Chirag Dilli,[4] he killed Ganju (a popular goon). Other famous goons also go to visit him and pay their respects to him. His son is now next in line. I have their support. When I was in school, if by mistake I would bump into someone, I would get slapped. Till Class 10 I was in Sarvodaya school. I would get easily intimidated at that time. Then one day my father told me about this uncle of mine; after that I realized I have 'force' behind me. After completing Class 11, whoever would misbehave with me, I would deal with him

---

[4] An authorized colony in South Delhi.

appropriately. My two cousin brothers who are in the same school, no one dares to misbehave with them because everybody knows that they are my brothers.

Easy access to drugs and alcohol could be reasons for feeling a part of a group, lending to strengthening of the alternate 'collective identity'. But Sonu's transition is from one who used to be scared earlier to one who boasts about how his brothers now use his name to feel protected in their school. This circle of networks, that allows protection and safety to enjoy mobility, is not one that everyone prescribes to. Yet, some do.

Much like Sonu, Aman, who also lives in Dakshinpuri, is aware of his social standing in the male groups here. He recounts his father's journey to us,

When my father came here he had a good muscular body. Sunny and Bobby were his friends. He was called 'Jitu bhai'. When we were really young my maternal grandmother fell sick. So, my father sent us (sisters and him) and my mother to be with her in the village. He used to stay here alone then. He had the freedom to roam around with his friends. He never got involved with alcohol or drugs but got involved in fights, etc. But there is a difference between the fights that happened back then and the ones that happen now. Earlier they would reach a compromise, now they just end up killing each other. They used to come for my father's birthday, so I've met everyone; they all know I'm Jitu *bhai*'s son. In fact, they all came on their bikes to escort me till the centre now. Everyone was staring!

Aman's other consistent narrative revolves around the many girlfriends he has had and the access to money he has. Now with a debit card at his disposal, which has been given to him by the company where he works, and the unquestioned mobility that being gainfully employed has brought with it, he enjoys the label of *ustaad* which has been given to him by his friends.

Afsana, who lives in Sanjay Camp, shares her relationship with her brother and her worries regarding his safety. She begins by reflecting that her father's journey resembles that of Aman's father.

> When my father came here, he was a local goon. Earlier girls were not allowed to wear jeans here. If a girl was seen with a boy, my father and other men like him would beat up the boy and take the girl to her house. If they spotted a girl wearing jeans, they would go to her house and inform her parents. People respected them too. He used to drink too. Once these men got married, they all went their separate ways. My mother has really improved him.

Her fear for her brother adds to this concept of the formation of the 'collective'. She says,

> He is the youngest of us all. He does not have any friends in our lane; they are all outsiders. His friends are much older than him, 22 years old! My biggest work is to go looking for him. I find him near the masjid, where all these boys just sit around on their bikes the entire day. He is young, so everyone beats him up. And he never tells us about it. We ask him if he has been threatened not to tell anyone, but he does not utter a word. People from outside come and inform us that he has been beaten up on that day. We are all scared for our brother and for our father. My father had a bad temper earlier. He would get easily involved in fights, and so on. Since our mother died he has changed immensely. He doesn't fight with anyone; instead, he apologizes because he knows

his children are alone at home. We don't have a support system without him here.

The *mahoul* (environment) here is bad. Big boys go around beating the younger ones; they ask them to do odd jobs for them. Therefore, I was saying that I'm scared for my brother. I'd rather have him watch television the entire day as opposed to him going out. I have to really control him. He doesn't even study anymore because he keeps loitering outside. We are going to put him in a hostel now. Both my sisters are working so they are outside most of the day. He doesn't listen to me. Only when my father is at home, he listens to him. None of us hit him because he is our one and only brother. I have been beaten up a lot in my childhood; our mother kept us disciplined. We were scared of her. He has always been told that 'he is the only son'; this idea has crept into his mind, that he is the only one, so no one can hit him. He has become more spoilt because of this. He fears our eldest sister; she's to him what our mother was for me.

Fear for their brothers, especially those who are younger than them, is a fear shared by most of the girls. Some curtail their brothers' mobility to safeguard them from the *mahoul* here, while others transfer them to private schools hoping the crowd there will be different.

CONCLUSION

In this chapter, we have tried to understand the lives of these young people through the lens of masculinity. This is a particularly important consideration as our participants live in close proximity to the malls and are surrounded by a capitalist media culture, both of which proclaim and facilitate consumption as a way of being. Possessing the latest model of phone, wearing branded clothes, going to the malls and taking selfies to be able to post on Facebook or WhatsApp—all of this forms a substantial part of how these young people, particularly boys, want to shape their identity in accordance to their growing aspirations.

What is the role of masculinity in this lifestyle based on consumption? With education, as is evident from the sharing of all our participants, the drop-out rate among boys is increasing, while among the girls it is decreasing, with some girls even going on to college. So, the question arises once again—is there a correlation between the increasing rate of drop-outs amongst boys and their masculinity? Do boys have fears about loitering in public spaces? In trying to answer this question, we have looked at masculinity via the lens of vulnerability and fear and attempted to deepen the understanding between the interlinkages of masculinity and violence, especially in the context of the formation of adolescent masculinities.

7

Masculinity and Violence

When I was in the school near Sohna Road, I was the only Valmiki, the rest were all jaat-gujjars. They used to roam around in groups while I was the only one from my community. One day, one of them harassed my older sister's friend. I beat them up. Then they got more people to beat me up from outside the school. I also got people from Khanpur. Since that day I have become brave (*mera jigra khul gaya*). My uncle introduced me to a goon who lives in Devligaon. He gave me his number and asked me to call him if I was in a problem. When 4–5 boys are standing in front of you, you cannot do anything alone. You need support.

Sonu, 20 years

In this chapter, we look at different aspects of violence in these resettlement colonies, the everydayness of violence here and its impact on the gendered reality; our focus here is therefore not political or communal violence. It is important to note that neither during the period of our fieldwork nor in the narratives that were shared by the participants did anyone talk about episodes of political or communal violence. But the everydayness of structural violence was too conspicuous to not look into more carefully.

This form of structural violence has levels; it becomes more pervasive as we go down the ladder of hierarchy. Thus, people living in a resettlement colony will face discrimination at multiple levels—who are the people who live in such spaces? What is their caste and class composition? What comprises their daily struggles of survival? From getting water to ensuring their homes are not inundated with sewage water, from saving money to running their household to saving enough so that their children can afford good private education. Standke-Erdmann (2001), a psychoanalyst, discusses the impact of this structural violence on individuals and observes, '…the entrenched structural violence generates personal violence… an omnipotent potential for conflicts exists, originating from the asymmetric power balances in the system. Where physical violence is one reaction to structural violence.'

This aspect has earlier been explored in Chapter 2 which looks at our participants' views on state and citizenship. But its impact on individual lives, with the sense of hopelessness that it can lead to, is felt on a day-to-day basis. Standke-Erdmann adds, '(there is an) overwhelming feeling of being up against an anonymous, huge, powerful creature called the System and to be confronted daily with the sharp contrast between power and powerlessness.' The boys and girls whom we spoke to continue to hold on to the threads of education because they know that education is their only asset which could help them break out of this cycle of helplessness and powerlessness.

With the boys however, it is more complicated. On the one hand are the structural discriminations that make it difficult for these boys to find employment, and on the other is the personal quest to reach the adult ideal of masculinity, measured in terms of work, marriage and where they stand in the social order. And they are found wanting—inferior to and dependent on adults. They look, therefore, to asserting their masculinity often through violence. In India where there is boundless emphasis on the male youth to be employed on the one hand and the lack of social structures to actualize these on the other, it invariably leads to resentment and powerlessness within the individual. Belonging to a 'collective identity' in such a situation gives a feeling of security to the individual.

There are clear examples in the stories shared by the young people here, where masculinity is wounded when young men are unable to find work that will provide for the family, even though reasons are structural and beyond their control. Violence then becomes the means through which a new kind of masculinity can be achieved.

Masculinity, Mobility and Fear

Phadke, Khan and Ranade's (2011) work on women's mobility and access to public space, makes us focus on the need to look at access to public space from a right to risk framework as opposed to a right to safety and protection framework. In addition to this, we argue that access to public space is also restricted for a certain kind of men, the 'masculine' type only. In Dakshinpuri and Sanjay Camp, forming a 'collective identity' or becoming a part of such groups becomes imperative to freely enjoy the public space. The ones who choose not to, have to restrict their own mobility for the fear of their safety. Over the last few years, families too have become acutely aware of this changing dynamic and have begun laying down boundaries for their sons and when and how they can access the public spaces. Girls and boys are navigating these restrictions in their own ways.

During the FGDs, boys and girls at different points shared their fears of loitering in public areas. While the girls were very vocal about their shared fears of being seen in public or being sexually harassed by the boys, only a few boys were willing to open up about their fears about living here. In the individual interviews, we specifically asked if the boys thought that girls have any fears of living here? To this Shekhar responded,

> Here, if a girl has a boyfriend, she is safe. If she is married, she is safe. Today, the way these girls are loitering around in the name of going for tuitions, it won't take too long to take them behind Virat.[1] The moment a girl steps out of her house, she has to face 30 boys. But she is not scared anymore. There is the Mahila Panchayat here, and the police also take strict actions now. If she complains to a nearby *bhaiyya*, he will gather more people and beat him up. Or she can dial 100. With so many facilities for her, how is she unsafe? What is the worry?

The question then arises, is a girl then responsible for her own safety?

The response we got was that she is safe, if she is in a relation-ship with a man, but if she is enjoying loitering or moving about on her own, her safety is threatened. In other words, a girl cannot access the public space until she has a purpose or is protected by her male counterparts.

---

[1] Virat, a defunct cinema hall, is infamous for being used by courting couples, especially young boys and girls.

Girls in the interview too shared and agreed with the latter half of Shekhar's statement that they do feel safer because of the presence of the Mahila Panchayat and the police as tools to at least threaten the boys with. But how many of them actually use these, is another question altogether.

Mahila Panchayat

Raj worked with the Mahila Panchayat for several years as a young boy. He shared his experience of it,

> Yesterday itself I saw a man beat up his wife. But we didn't say anything. We don't know them. People usually retort saying that it is their family matter. Then one feels like there is no point in trying to help the other person. Thus, nobody interferes anymore. The next day, some might go over to their house and inquire if all is well. If families are unable to resolve it among themselves, then there is the Mahila Panchayat or the police. Women from ASHA come to do the investigation. If it can get resolved at this level it is ok. If not, then the case is forwarded to the family district court. Once I grew older, I was prohibited to attend these meetings so now I don't know how they function.

On the whole, the boys we spoke to were empathic and mindful of the correlation between the perceived danger and risks for girls and the restrictions on their mobility. They said,

> Girls are unable to say anything to a boy because they fear the kind of person he might turn out to be. Girls are allowed to go only to school and for tuitions. They can't loiter much. The ones who reach college, they learn ways to commute. Others are confined to their houses or at the most to their relatives' houses; not the way boys can loiter. Now, even if a

boy or a girl is just roaming around all by him/her self, people will presume that he/she is going to meet someone. There is *ched-chad* too, which is another cause of fear for girls.

Some boys are accustomed to teasing girls, even if she is with her parents. But what happens is, the parents will blame their daughter because they presume that she knows that random boy: why would a random boy otherwise talk to a girl? The suspicion is always on the girl. If the family is nice, they might ask her and clarify things too. If the suspicion builds, the family might marry her off early or prohibit her from going outside and enrol her in open schooling instead.

In the same chain of thought, Sandeep shared, 'Yes, girls have fears; I've seen them getting sexually harassed. Therefore, they don't leave their homes mostly, only the ones who have a job do.'

Aman added to this,

When boys don't feel safe, how will the girls? The moment she reaches Dakshinpuri, she calls her friend or parents to come pick her up. But her biggest fear is that if someone will see her talking to a boy, even if he is her brother! They will inform her parents and then they will beat her up and prohibit her from leaving her house to even go to school or for tuitions.

When girls are seen in public, especially with a boy, it is she who is questioned, and in keeping with this societal attitude, it is she who is blamed if and when she is sexually harassed. Going to a school or having a job does give more freedom to the girls, but they need the protection of male company to be able to afford this mobility.

Sandeep felt that girls cannot have fears because their mobility is already restricted.

No, girls have no fears because they rarely leave their homes. And even when they do it is in the daytime to go to the market to buy something, till about 8–8:30 when there are people outside. Girls don't go out at night, only boys do. After that, there are fewer people on the streets and if she needs to go out she needs to be with someone, brother, older sister, aunt. She cannot go out unaccompanied.

When she is younger, she is allowed to go out, but as she grows into adolescence, she's not allowed to; then she has to stay at home. I don't know why this happens, but my mother tells me that it's useless for girls to go out…boys abduct girls, make their videos, dishonour them. Thus no one sends their girls outside, and when they do, she needs to go with someone older. My younger sister goes out but with her friends. My mother can go out alone, she's older, no one dare say anything to her, she will deal with them sternly.

There is a vicious cycle in operation here—girls and their families fear a loss of honour if she is sexually harassed. This leads to restrictions on her mobility and because there is restriction on her mobility in place already, she will not fear anything because she is protected within the walls of the house. The age factor complicates this further. When a girl reaches puberty, she is considered to be sexually mature and hence needs to be protected. This fear, of being seen publicly, was echoed by most girls in their narratives as well. While the fear of sexual harassment still exists, they are also learning ways to overcome their fears and are determined to question this imbalance. After one of the FGDs, we asked the girls if they were given a chance to ask the boys something, what would their questions be. Almost instantly and vociferously, as if they were waiting to be asked to do this, they charged with the following:

> We'll ask them why do you harass girls? Why do you have so much attitude? Where do you get the courage from, the power to hold anyone's hand as and when you please, what is the deal? You have the freedom to make girlfriends, but when your sister has a boyfriend then what is your problem? Why do you keep commenting on everyone, including aunties and uncles?

Unfortunately, we could not arrange for a space where the boys and girls could talk to each other, but it did remind us that we needed to understand the 'why' behind each of these questions more critically. Deepti Priya Mehrotra (2001) explores the reason behind why men are aggressive through the critique of a film in her article; she writes, 'we need to treat "violent" men as victims of their conditioning—not just as criminals. Of course, at one level, there is no excuse for violent behaviour. But we must understand why it happens and be able to make meaningful interventions.'

We asked the girls if they had fears about living here?

Nazrana shared how she used to be out all day long and had to be persuaded to stay at home as a child. But as she grew up, she began feeling unsafe and restricted her own mobility,

> What if today I say something to that boy (who has harassed me on the streets) and tomorrow if he finds me alone, I don't know what he's capable of doing. I prefer staying at home now. I have thought this through; I am going to ask Allah to make me a boy in my next birth—I won't have to wash utensils, I can take my own decisions. At home though, my

father says that boys and girls are equal but, in their practices, they end up differentiating! Like, my brothers are never questioned about why they are wearing jeans. They can never be questioned! But if I wear jeans, then I am questioned. And why before our marriage we are not allowed to have a phone? I think if someone has to use a phone, they can borrow it from their friends also!

Aarti echoes the exasperation articulated by the other girls on being discriminated against because one is born a girl.

I feel very scared. Even now while coming here I ran straight to the centre. I don't like going out alone. My father doesn't allow me either. If someone passes a comment aimed at me, I ignore it and keep walking. My mother has told me to ignore such comments, and in case there is a problem she has told me that I should call them. They keep calling to check on me while I'm outside. This makes me very angry with them. My brother has the password to my Facebook account. He does check my account from time to time. It's ok. Sometimes I feel angry that he can check my phone, but I can't check his. But what can I do, he's my older brother; if I'll say something to him he will hit me. The other reason is that girls fear being seen while talking to a boy here. Everyone knows everyone in Dakshinpuri. My mother has also warned me about this. Even if we have friends who are boys, we'll talk to them at the tuition centre only but not outside on the streets. I don't always tell the truth to my parents about my whereabouts; I don't share everything with my mother. Like I will never tell my mother about *ched-khani*. I feel if I tell her she will only blame me for it.

Aarti's surveillance by her brother and mother is a symbol of the lack of trust they have in her. She in turn, reciprocates by hiding the details about her whereabouts from her mother. What could be the effects on one's psyche when one grows up observing gender-based discrimination in one's home, is unable to question it, and feels the mistrust there between family members?

The other side of the story is taking the risk to loiter in public spaces and finding ways to counter the sexual harassment, as shared by Priya and Zoya in their interviews.

Priya is the youngest of three sisters. Her mother works as a domestic help while her father has been struggling with alcohol addiction and subsequent unemployment. She shared with us,

> I used to get scared earlier but not anymore; now I give a befitting reply if they pass a comment. But there are some whom I still fear, like the ones who are older or who are drunk. You find these groups of boys in every *gali*. Now I share at home also, earlier I wouldn't. I've seen my sisters and friends do the same, so I also learnt it from them. One day this boy passed a comment aimed at me so I replied in turn; he apologized to me then! That is when I realized that if I give an appropriate response they might keep quiet and not do it again. But if I say something wrong then he might react in an aggressive way. Thus, one needs to be mindful of what to say. I do feel scared about how he might react. Girls do loiter outside, but they have timings, like by 8 or 9 most are expected to be back home. I sit outside with my paternal grandmother and aunt in our *gali* till 11 at night watching videos and cracking jokes.

Meera, who works with the NGO has attended many trainings on prevention of sexual violence and laws related to it. She said to us, 'I threaten the boys right away. I tell them I know the laws and will lodge a complaint against them. We are taught that we need to put a stop to such behaviour the first time itself.'

Afsana firmly refutes our question,

No, nobody harasses me. People fear me. I look at people
and they don't do anything. My sister keeps telling me to
ignore them. How much can one ignore? One day this ignorance is going to break its boundaries. One day we were
coming home and this boy commented that we were looking
nice. I replied saying that you are not looking nice. My sister
scolded me for doing so. I don't like people commenting
about me and me keeping quiet when they do so. I like going
to the big park here or to the markets like Sarojini Nagar,
Lajpat Nagar and Madangir market with my friends.

It became evident to us that whether it is about a verbal reply or
a threat of the police, girls are questioning the absolute authority
and presence of men in the public space and taking the risk to
claim the streets as their own.

We next asked the girls if they thought that the boys had any
fears about living here? They responded by saying that they did
recognize that boys had fears regarding their safety as well, in
particular, about getting dragged into brawls, even murder, and
they reiterated to us that all this happens more at night. But
overall, the girls did not think that the boys had any fears about
living in the locality.

Boys are scared, but they don't show it.
They have no fears; they are fearless. They have no prob-
lems. Since they are boys they have been given all the free-
dom; even to loiter at night without any fear. Our mothers
also side with them and defend them. But their only fear is if
their family gets to know about any of their girlfriends. Even
then, they will be restricted to not leaving their house for 2–3
days; but for the girls it becomes a bigger problem. They are
not scared of the police either; they are out sexually harassing
girls on the streets openly.

Afsana added rather eloquently,

> Why would boys fear anything? They keep loitering around.
> Take my brother for example; he is not aware how his future
> is going to get spoilt because of what he is doing today. We
> are older, we know this. He enjoys loitering around, living
> here and talking to his friends. Nobody fears anything.

It was interesting for us to note that the girls' comments were
in stark opposition to the vulnerabilities that were shared by the
boys regarding their own fears.

Do Boys have Fears about Living Here?

Varun was among the quietest ones during the FGDs. He would
be given the role of a timid woman during a play and would
always respond with 'what do I say about this, ask others' when
we tried to ask him how he felt about it. We were surprised with
the comfort with which he could share his vulnerabilities and
fears with us during the individual interviews.

> I don't go out alone, I need someone's company. People drive
> very fast here, I'm scared of their speed. I don't know the roads
> here too well, what if I wander off? After my Class 12 I have
> started going out alone. I'm scared at night. In the daytime I
> can go anywhere. Or if it's *sunsaan* then I get scared. I'm very
> scared of fights. I fear that it might be lead to something more.
> I get nervous/palpitations, my heartbeat increases. If I see
> someone fight, I go as far from there as I can and return only
> once things are calm again. At home, only my brothers fight
> with each other. But outside, that is what I fear. I don't know
> what happens to me, but I feel tense. His voice changes as he
> contemplatively narrates this.

Varun aspires to become a guide but he is well aware of his
limitations that might hinder actually realizing this aspiration:

I want to become a guide. I need to learn English for that though. I like to travel. I am interested in this. You need to know many languages to become a guide. Sometimes I feel I will not be able to do it. Maybe I will do something else then, like get a good job. I have seen these guides at places like Humayun's Tomb. I have never talked to any of them though, I feel scared. I have seen guides on Discovery Channel too. My brother thinks I should learn English first. But I can't find a good teacher. Or a place where there are fewer students. I hope I master working on computers well. I keep applying online for jobs. There is a woman teacher where I go to learn computers. I am scared to ask her anything. Now I do because I am the only student in her class and there are no girls with me. Sometimes I don't meet my friends for days. I don't leave my house for many days. Even now the fear hasn't completely gone: fear of talking to girls, fear of going anywhere outside. My family scolds me a lot about this. I like living in quiet/silence. I just don't like loud noises. I like winters because no one leaves their house to come out. If guests come home, I greet them and leave.

Varun's heightened fear of space and girls could be due to other reasons as well which we were unable to understand within the scope of this research. But his fear of speaking to girls was voiced by other male participants as well. Like Prakash who feared being 'beaten up with a sandal' if he approached a girl even to be a friend. Or Sandeep who feels that post the 16 December 2012 gangrape in Delhi, girls feel more empowered to approach the police if they feel threatened or offended. This has made many boys fearful for their own safety with respect to knowing that their communication with girls could be misread and it could lead to a police case for sexually harassing a girl. This fear of the police increased post August 2017 when Section 144[2] was implemented here.

Possible Reasons behind the Violence

During the course of our research, two things were recurrent across themes and across interviews. The first is the role that the markets, especially with the proximity of these localities to the malls, play in the lives of our young participants. The second is the increased use of phones and the Internet. As described earlier, the aspiration to purchase and consume the mall culture is immense with both boys and girls, but more so with the boys.

Surajchand was perhaps the only one who has been very sceptical of the consumer culture and the widespread growth and use of media. He reminisced to us about his childhood when everyone played together outside in the streets and parks and was pained with the changes that he had observed growing up in his neighbourhood.

> Since people used to roam around the streets, they knew where what was, the bus stand for example. Having a phone has created distances between people. But the ones who are physically away have become closer! People would rather play on the Internet with strangers. Because we played with each other there was interaction with the other. Now no one even sits with anyone. People have labelled Dakshinpuri and Sanjay Camp as bad (bura). What has happened is that over

---

[2] Section 144 of the Criminal Procedure Code (CrPC) of 1973 empowers an executive magistrate to prohibit an assembly of more than four persons in an area. According to 141-149 of the Indian Penal Code (IPC), the maximum punishment for engaging in rioting is rigorous imprisonment for three years and/or fine.

a period of time people living here have accepted this label. Ok we are bad! Kids here have access to weapons also. And then there is YouTube; people post their videos just so that they can become famous; *apna rubaab dikhana hota hai.* They commit a murder, and someone will upload it online but will not help the one who is being murdered.

Saying this, he sighs in a resigned manner.

Priya helped us understand this changing social landscape from another perspective. Nobody used to think that girls and boys playing together is bad. We used to loiter outside till 11 at night. Now we can't even stand in the balcony! In my childhood I had many boys who were my friends. We used to play all kinds of games together. But when I turned 10 or 11, everybody started saying that we have grown up now and should focus on studies rather than on play.

This disruption in friendships with the opposite sex was felt sharply by everyone. Some boys, like Aman, recognize that while they can form intimate relationships, they are not in the habit of letting their sisters do so.

Prakash had remarked during one of our discussions,

...(with respect to the need for co- education) now there is no point. Nothing is going to change. What is happening now is that if a boy, even by mistake, speaks to a girl, and if by chance her brother or even brother's friend sees them he is not going to ask or say anything. He'll just start beating him. Murders too happen because of this. If from the beginning we had co-education, then all this would not have happened. She's a girl, I'm a boy—everything would be normal. When things are hidden, then it leads to such events.

There is of course no guarantee that co-education would solve the issues of patriarchy, but it could at least create a window of opportunity to understand each other a little more. Our research did not focus on the impact of media on the violence in these resettlement colonies. Whether the reel impacts the real or vice-versa, one cannot conclusively say. But there is an undeniable impact of the growing consumer culture on how we understand ourselves and the others around us.

The Role of Authority in the Face of Violence and No Safety

Shekhar's lens

At 22, Shekhar is the oldest in the group. He has completed his BA. He lives with his older brother, parents and his father's sister. His father came to Dakshinpuri in the 1980s and works as a data operator at AIIMS.[3] Shekhar is currently working in the administration department of Delhi Public School in Saket. He is called 'bhai' by all the participants and we observed that his opinions invariably swayed those of the group.

Speaking of a recent incident where a resident was killed in police custody, he says,

> This is all political. It is a political game. It all depends on how much you bribe the police with. Only the language of money is understood here, nothing else. Why was that boy killed inside the prison cell? Because all the policemen were bribed, including the SHO. Why would the hawaldar give a rod to another prison mate? All the policemen were sent out

---

[3] All India Institute of Medical Sciences in South Delhi.

on the pretext of getting water, the other prison mates were also sent out. He hit that boy with that rod and killed him.

Shekhar is evidently dismayed by the police and the corrupt politics of the city. Similar versions of this incident were shared by each participant.

In a similar vein, during our discussions, Rohini intensely critiqued the MCD[4] department of the government.

The government under the garb of making everyone equal is only trying to propagate India as a brand. Only a few can move ahead in this; while the rich are getting richer the poor are getting poorer. The government is interested only in building its status by increasing its capital. I don't think the government is able to run this country well. I know it is difficult to run such a big country. But it can happen slowly. Like demonetization—I can't see what use or benefit came from it. What was its use or benefit, I can't understand! It is strange what they are doing. The impact of demonetization here was very bad. Some people died, many weddings got cancelled. In the beginning we thought black money would be recovered, but I think everybody had already hidden it. Everybody was angry.

It is fairly evident to us that the systemic corruption that Shekhar observed in the police force, was observed by Rohini in another level of the government, the MCD. She clearly identifies corruption in the ways in which the government through its economic policies is pretending to work towards the promise of development for the poor but is only instead working for the rich and to enhance their profits further.

[4] Municipal Corporation of Delhi.

The Police and Section 144: Creating More Fear

One of the questions we discussed was regarding the role of the police in either creating or curbing the structural violence prevalent in these localities? The implementation of Section 144 of the IPC in the face of day-to-day violence or internal community conflicts had a deep impact on the boys here. While it reduced the fear among the girls when it came to their capacity to access the public space, it made the boys feel extremely fearful of authority; to their mind, it jeopardized their personal safety. They felt it was a way for the police to make their presence felt.

Shekhar said to us about this,

The new SHO here has introduced the rule that if the police see any two boys standing together post 11 at night, they will be taken directly into custody. Their parents would then have to come, show enough IDs and have them released. Shops are also asked to shut by 10 at night. They came and arrested 30–40 boys just the other day. This is scary.

Surajchand begins with a rhetorical question,

What can the police do? On the one hand, they side with the goons and on the other I fear that they might imprison me based on a mere suspicion. I feel very scared. My parents also fear for us. They tell us not to be outside after 8 or 9 at night. If we get into a fight, it might become a police case. Parents have asked us not to invite our friends over, especially at night. In case something happens to them when they come to visit us, it will become our responsibility. It gets very tense here at night. I avoid areas where there are many people sitting together, in case they say something. I try never to be alone as well. The fear is from within that even when it is not our fault, one can't trust what the other might do.

From the grand and notorious representation of the police in Bollywood films that have tainted them as always being late to arrive at a crime scene, being corrupt and basically useless, to the same film industry that portrays them as the overtly masculine protectors of law and its citizens, our imagination of the role of the police may be coloured but not the expectation we have from them. The expectation is clear—to protect the people of the country without any biases or discrimination. However, that is not what young boys think the police does for them. They feel intensely vulnerable and helpless when it comes to the police and hold the firm belief that the police favours only powerful people with political connections. The expectation from the police to be fair and just does not exist in their system.

Shekhar shares what he thinks is the ineptness of the system,

> The police are corrupt, they are concerned with only making money. A murder took place inside a prison! One of the accused paid the police and murdered his enemy inside the prison. The police take money from the shopkeepers here and even from pick-pocketers. When they are taking money from the pick-pocketers themselves, why would they stop crime being committed? The police, as a whole, is scared of the big gangsters here. They arrest the innocent and take money to free the gangsters instead.

Alok shared an incident when his oldest brother was taken into custody. He called his neighbour who works in the NDMC[5] for

---

[5] New Delhi Municipal Corporation.

help. When this failed to get his brother released, Alok called another known individual who works at the Prime Minister's residence. His brother was then released. But he was kept in custody till four in the morning. His brother had shown his IDs to the policemen and explained that he was only returning home from work but the police refused to believe him.

Anil and Sandeep both witnessed a murder that took place around April 2017, a little before Section 144 was implemented. They recounted how they saw a group of boys first beat up a boy and then shoot him to death. It happened near the main bus stand. Since they were both caught on the CCTV camera as eyewitnesses, their families were frightened and worried for their safety, both in terms of the threat posed by the goons who had committed the crime as well as the police. This happened on the day the two boys gave their Class 12 Maths exam; they were returning home after the examination. Following this incident, both their families restrained them from going out.

Another way in which such instances of violence spread is through the sharing of videos. In the case described above as well, a video was made recording this murder which was widely circulated. It is through such a video that Sandeep and Anil realized that they had been captured on the CCTV footage and could possibly be taken into custody by the police for questioning.

When Section 144 was imposed, many of the families put restrictions on their sons' mobility. They feared that their sons might be taken into custody for no fault of their own. Loitering in the daytime or outside Dakshinpuri and Sanjay Camp is still permissible, but wandering about at night is out of bounds.

Alok shared the fear for his older brother, 'He comes back from work around midnight or 1 AM. After 10 we call him every 15 minutes to check on him. Our father has instructed us not to react even if someone abuses us, to keep quiet and find our way home.

These words remind us of what the mothers have been telling their daughters all their life; with the girls, it is their sexuality and 'honour' that is challenged/questioned, but for the boys it is bodily harm, theft and even danger to one's life that needs to be safeguarded against. As a strategy the boys look for things that they can use to protect themselves with, like a stone that they can throw at an attacker and run away.

What the Imposition of Section 144 Meant for Girls

While the boys fear this law, the girls on the other hand wished that this law be implemented forever. Nazrana explained, 'The police would come patrolling every night at 10 and beat up all the boys who were out loitering. Not even one boy could be seen outside then as long as this rule was in place; now it is back to how it was before with groups of boys standing everywhere. The police don't care much when such a rule is not in place.

She extended this by explaining the role of the police through a gender lens,

The police are always suspicious about the girl's character, they question her background. They ask her questions like, 'do you have a boyfriend? Is the boy who teased you your ex- boyfriend?' They blame the girl. She can do as she wants in her personal life, what is their problem! How can they interfere in her personal life, question her character and check her background? The boys are never questioned. Even when they are outside the house for three days straight, nobody interferes in their personal lives. But when a girl is outside for even an hour she is questioned about her whereabouts. The police is also useless: you bribe them and they release you. This is wrong. The boys who commit crimes should be punished. Like the one who murdered someone inside the prison, he will be out soon. When murders happen inside the prison then how can one feel safe outside?

Shekhar and Nazrana raise some pertinent questions: Who is the police meant for? What are the repercussions of random implementation of certain laws? Why is the police more vigilant in one area and completely dismissive in another?

It is important for us to understand why such rules or laws get implemented. These are some of the responses we received:

We've seen fights right here beneath our house. We are scared as well. Mummy also tells us not to watch when this happens; they fight very badly. If there is enmity, they even knife each other.

If there are fights at home on some account, it ends up with persons beating each other. Husbands beat wives; nobody can ever step in and save the woman—they'll also get beaten up. If these conflicts occur outside the house people call up the police, but if there are fights inside the house, no one calls the police and no one interferes in a family matter.

There is a lot of loot. Just taking out a knife to take money. After drinking, nobody is in their senses; they just want to beat up someone. The biggest reason is intoxication and they could be high on anything; where there is intoxication, there will be violence.

The nexus between criminals and politicians is commonly regarded as an important reason why the cycle of violence does not end quickly. According to one of the young boys:

Earlier there was not so much crime; now for every little thing there is a crime. Earlier when there was a fight, sticks would be used; now bullets and knives fly. Crime is increasing .... partly because of the Sarkaar ... also movies; there's a lot of action shown in South Indian movies ... people think they will become famous also by doing all this ... there was one boy who used to wander the streets—he was a real *badmash* and he had a minister's backing. If you don't have political backing, then life is difficult.

The place of residence is an important aspect of the aspirations of young people living in these JJ clusters or resettlement colonies. They want to live in colonies where there is no crime, where the police is not so arbitrary in its actions, where basic facilities are provided so that they do not have to struggle even for their basic needs like water and the drainage system.

When I become something, I will leave this place. So many murders take place. Like my father gets drunk and we are so scared that he will be lying drunk somewhere, someone will rob him, some boys. Even when my uncle doesn't come home, we stand outside and wait—he is a chef and his cab comes to drop him, but still we worry. We can look after our own safety by not going out, but we fear for our family members.

It is ironic that police presence which is supposedly put in place to instil trust and a sense of safety among people, has created more fear and a deep sense of insecurity, especially among young boys. However, girls feel more secure with increased police presence and as seen above, even expressed the wish that

Section 144 be imposed permanently in their neighbourhood. Some of the girls even shared,

> If there is no security for boys, what will happen to the girls? When a girl enters Dakhshinpuri, she calls her parents or her friends and then goes with them. Then she doesn't want to get out of the house for the fear that if anyone sees her talking to a boy, whoever he may be, they will tell her family, her brother and everything will be stopped for her—school, tuition, just speaking with others—and that she will be locked in.

CONCLUSION

Masculinity cannot be read simply as what men do. Rather, this 'doing' needs be deconstructed in the particular context of the men under study and there is further a need to understand the reasons for how they behave.

There seems to be clear evidence from our research that girls in resettlement colonies like Dakshinpuri and Sanjay Park live through, question and understand the impositions of patriarchy on their lives. The boys, however, seem to be searching for questions in order to unpack their lives in the context of what is expected of them and what they want.

The question is whether we can give both girls and boys an opportunity and the space to make meaning of their respective and collective experiences, through the lens of gender and sexuality, so that the implications of patriarchal structures are not understood in isolation for girls/women, but also for boys/men and consequently the ripple effect on girls/women, and thus on everyone in the system. This is particularly important because the idea of masculinity not only shapes how boys should behave, act and perform, but also how girls should behave, act and perform vis-à-vis their roles in contrast to masculine roles. It also defines in certain ways how everyone else who does not fall within the binary of male and female is guided by the norms of masculinity.

As we have seen from the findings and voices in the preceding pages, class and caste cast their shadow over almost every aspect of the lives of people in these localities: from the aspirations of the young who are acutely conscious of the class divide which leads to state neglect and poor infrastructure to an inability to bridge the difference and socialize with an upper class, an inability to afford better education, better jobs and a better lifestyle. They hold their lower class status responsible for all their ills and wretchedness, and their future, almost always, is about raising their status to a higher class, almost always by earning more and affording all the things they associate with a more privileged class—from clubs and shopping in malls to better homes, and a life in 'Gurgaon, or Singapore or Dubai'. Despite this, however, and in one way, fuelled by their prejudices arising out of their own predicament, they discriminate against those who they think belong to a lower class than even themselves (and there are enough class differences that dominate Dakshinpuri and Sanjay Camp). Further, their sense of self-worth is often boosted by being perceived as someone of a higher class based on what they own and what they can afford. The yearning to close the class gap is also hugely influenced by spatial discrimination, urbanized neighbours, media representations, social media and state neglect.

8

Conclusion

The people living in Dakshinpuri and Sanjay Camp felt a strong sense of otherization. The way otherization functions here is in two ways. One is based on class—that between a Saket and a Sanjay Camp—and the other is based on caste within Dakshinpuri and Sanjay Camp. Sandeep's perception of his context and that of others living in more affluent places like Saket is evident when he shares his future dreams of living in Saket or Gurgaon. He says,

> Good people go to malls, not like people from here. Like people from Saket, NOIDA, Gurgaon, CP. When I go to malls I meet them, we greet each other with a 'hi-hello'. I enjoy talking to them. They talk politely unlike people living here. When we share with them that we live in Dakshinpuri, they tell us that it doesn't look like it. We sometimes take pictures with them. People don't maintain cleanliness here, some do, but not others, like Valimikis. They rear pigs, spread dirt, I find them *bekaar* (useless). A garbage truck comes there (Saket) daily to collect garbage, here (in our area) it comes rarely. People wash their clothes daily there, here people go without changing their clothes for four or five days

at times. I dream of being educated and of becoming a good person. I will then live in a nice place like Gurgaon or Saket. I want to travel too but first I want to get a good job. My father sometimes says to me that I should travel but I feel I should study well first.

This reference to 'these people' (referring to people living in Sanjay Camp) and 'those people' (referring to people living in Saket) is found consistently in Sandeep's narrative. He distances himself from being included among 'these people' and wishes to become a part of 'those people'. Going to malls is a symbol of one's class status and when one does, one must look a certain way to be able to present themselves as a part of the group that visits malls regularly, and not look like where they actually come from.

Caste is deeply embedded in the historical discrimination brought by their parents from the villages and it continues to perpetuate itself, rearing its head to create challenges in relationships—friendship, love, marriage, at work and the kind of work they can do, in the resources available to them, and in the manifestation of violence and fear.

Many participants in our research associated 'dirt' with the Valmiki community. It is also a fact that Non-Valmiki participants do have friends who are Valmiki, they go to their homes and relish the non-vegetarian food cooked at their homes which is not allowed in their own. They have all grown up together. However, some feel that the violence and 'dirt' now character-izing the locality was brought to Dakshinpuri and Sanjay Camp by 'them', the Valmikis. Where is this otherization coming from? To begin with, it reflects the general perception of the Valmiki community in other parts of the country as well. One wonders, if friendships have broken the barriers of caste, then why do we hold on to these discriminatory narratives? The dichotomy here is that while Sandeep recognizes the failure of the state in the lack of water and garbage disposal facilities and the distinction between the poor and the rich, he uses that exact explanation to divide the two 'kinds'/'classes' of people present in his narrative—'they' wash their clothes daily, but people 'here' do not; even though this is a reality that stems more from lack of water, a structural failure of the government, than anything else. The otherization of mall people, and their (cleanliness) superiority, is seen as a result of structural differences, while the otherization of the Valmikis and their (un-cleanliness) and inferiority is seen as their own fault.

Like caste and class, gender creates its own dimensions of inequalities and discriminations. It not only affects education, work, mobility, safety and choices for the future, the different lenses through which boys and girls look at the same theme, its reality and the future demonstrate different perspectives that constitute the whole. The tyranny of patriarchy is a challenge for both boys and girls. There is much that brings them together, and yet much divides them.

It has to be stated at this point that while gender norms are generally understood via the lens of feminism, it would be really interesting to explore them via the lens of masculinity and thus also understand feminism as an essential extension of masculinity or vice-versa. Femininity and masculinity actually feed each other to reinforce the gender and sexual norms imposed by social structures.

We conclude with a few probable questions that this research allowed us to understand and forced us to engage with.

- As people working in the development sector or otherwise, can we listen to the boys and their increased sense of being invisibilized? And do so by not denying the need for sustained efforts towards girl empowerment, instead ensuring that this time the 'other' side is not left behind creating ruptures and fragments of a different kind in the movement towards gender equity.

- Can we listen to the changing landscape of gender and address the various contradictions that emerge in how girls and boys understand themselves and each other? The need perhaps is to create those spaces where sharing of one's own narratives and listening to those of others is enabled. In the consumer culture that we all exist in, it is not feasible to live without market-oriented aspirations. But with the added failure and apathy of the state, what could be the long-term impact of this on the lives of these young people?

- Our participants have been born and brought up in Delhi, hence their experience of migration is more intra-state as opposed to inter-state, and thus migration never surfaced as a theme to be engaged with. But what role does migration play in the larger socio-political-economic discourse? How will they address the deeply embedded challenges of class and caste which are responsible for discrimination as much as gender and spatial structures?

- In the bigger picture, the structural discrimination is about economic class and caste, both of which are reflected in every aspect of the lives of these young people, their environment, their community and their engagement with all stakeholders. Their voices are hopeful, their aspirations are mirrored in the media and their urbanized neighbourhood, and yet do their fears and reality sound like they will be robbed of their dreams?

Annexures

Annexure 1 *District Map of Delhi*

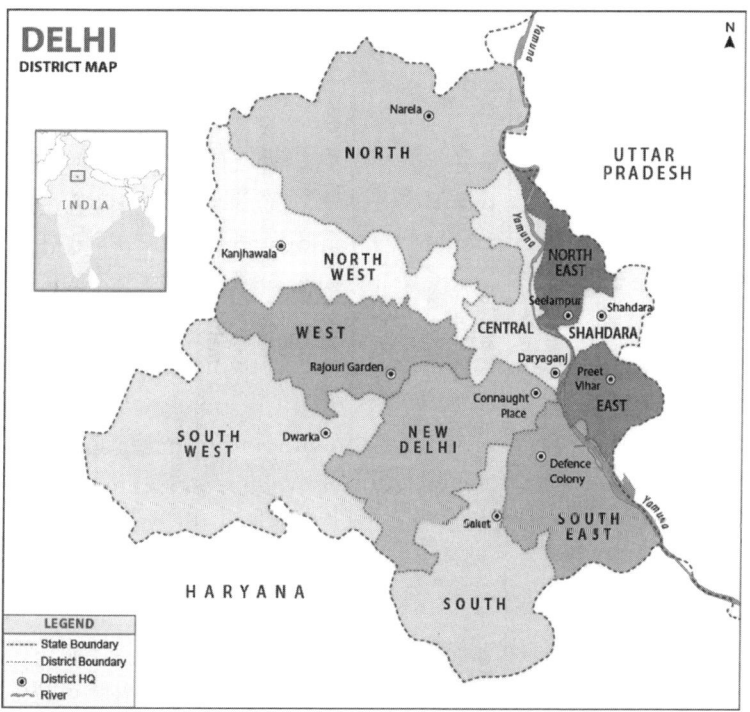

Source: https://commons.wikimedia.org/wiki/File:Delhi_district_map.jpg
Credit: Aakash Singh

Annexure 2 Research Participant Profiles

Names	Age	Education	Caste	Parents Education and Work Profile	Siblings Education and Work Profile
Sandeep	18	12th pass. Pursuing CMA course	Koli	Father studied till class 5 and works as foreman. Mother is illiterate and is housewife	He has one younger sister. She is studying in 11th class.
Vijay	19	Graduated	SC	Both his parents are illiterate. Father works with NDMC. Mother is housewife.	4 brothers and 2 sisters. One brother and sister are married. Elder brothers are graduates and are working. Younger sister is in 10th class.
Shekhar	22	Graduated and working with administration in Delhi Public School.	SC	Father is 12th pass and works as data operator in AIIMS. Mother is 8th pass and is housewife. But she participates in Mahila Panchayat in Dakshinpuri	1 brother and 2 sisters. Sisters are married and studied till 12th. Brother has graduated.
Sonu	20	Pursuing B.Sc from open university	Valmiki	Father is CA. Mother is illiterate and is housewife.	One sister who is also in last year of her college.
Prakash	20	Graduated	Berua	Father is 12th pass and is electrician. Mother is illiterate and is housewife.	1 elder brother and 1 elder sister. Sister studied till 10th and is married. Brother is working.

Name	Age	Education	Caste	Parents	Siblings
Anil	18	12th pass. Pursuing CMA course		Father is 10th pass and is electrician. Mother is 5th pass and housewife.	He has 3 brothers. 1 is studying in 10th class and other is in 6th class. One brother drooped out of school and is a mechanic.
Aman	18	12th pass		Father is 10th pass and works as Foreman. Mother is 8th pass and is housewife.	3 sisters. Two are school-going—one in 10th class and other in 9th class. One is 12th pass and she is working in Action India.
Alok	22	Graduated	Kohli	Father is 10th pass and runs a vegetable shop. Mother is illiterate and is housewife.	2 elder brothers who are working. Surajchand is his younger brother. 2 younger sister who are school-going.
Surajchand	21	Graduated	Kohli	Father is 10th pass and runs a vegetable shop. Mother is illiterate and is housewife.	2 elder brothers who are working. Alok is his elder brother. 2 younger sister who are school-going.
Ajay	18	Studying in 12th class	Valmiki	His mother is a political party worker.	
Rohini	18	Pursuing BA from open university. Working as data operator in a store.	SC	Both her mother and father are 10th pass. Her mother is housewife. And her father runs a clothes shop.	She has an elder brother who is also pursuing BA. Two younger sisters and both are school-going.

Names	Age	Education	Caste	Parents Education and Work Profile	Siblings Education and Work Profile
Komal	15	Studying in class 10th	SC	Doesn't have parents as she lives with her maternal grandparents.	
Pinky	15	Studying in class 10th	SC	Father is 12th pass and does some private job. Mother is illiterate and is housewife.	2 elder sisters and 1 elder brother. All of them are 12th pass. One sister and brother work in some shop in nearby market. One sister doesn't work outside home.
Priya	15	Studying in class 10th	SC	Father is 7th pass and works as labourer. Mother is 3rd pass and is housewife.	One brother and two sisters. All are school going.
Charu	17	12th pass	Valmiki	Father is 12th pass and does some private job. Mother is 12th pass and is housewife.	2 brothers and 1 sister. One brother is working and he is married. Sister is pursuing BCA. Youngest brother is in school.
Nazrana	16	Pursuing 10th from open university.	Manihar	Father is 12th pass and runs a bakery.	

Name	Age	Education/Work		Parents	Siblings
Aarti	16	Studying in 11th class		Father is 10th pass and works as fieldworker in Delhi metro. Mother is 7th pass and is housewife.	One elder brother who is in college. One younger sister who is studying in 9th class.
Afsana	17	Studying in 12th class	ST	Father is 10th pass and works as painter.	2 elder sisters. One is working and one doesn't works outside. Younger brother is studying in class 5.
Zoya	19	Working in Action India. And pursuing BA from open university.		Mother is illiterate and is housewife.	3 elder sisters and all are married. 1 elder brother and is working.
Anita	16	Studying in class 11th		Father is graduated and works as an English teacher in a govt school. Mother is housewife.	One younger brother and one younger sister. Both are school-going.

Annexure 3 *Profile and Consent Form*

प्रोफाइल

दिनांक: _____

1. आपका नाम: _____

2. आपकी उम्र: _____

3. माँ का नाम: _____

   पिता का नाम: _____

   भाई का नाम: _____

   बहन का नाम: _____

4. आपका पता: _____

5. आप किस जाति के हैं? नीचे उसके सामने सही का निशान लगाएं

1 अनुसूचित जाति (SC)
2 अनुसूचित जनजाति (ST)
3 अन्य पिछड़ वर्ग (OBC)

6. आपका धर्म: _____

7. अभी आपकी वैवाहिक स्थिति क्या है? किसी एक पर टिक करें।
1. शादी शुदा [_]
2. अविवाहित [_]
3. विधवा [_]
4. तलाकशुदा या पति से अलग. [_]

8. आप मूल निवासी किस राज्य की हैं। _____

9. आप संजय कैंप में कब से रह रहे हैं? _____

10. माँ का रोज़गार _____
पिता का रोज़गार _____
क्या आप किसी रोज़गार से जुड़े हैं _____

11. आप किस कक्षा में पढ़ रहे हैं? _____

12. अपने स्कूल के अनुभव के बारे में थोड़ा बताएं: _____

13. परिवार के सदस्यों की शौक्षिक स्थिति

पिता – अशिक्षित /शिक्षित, अगर शिक्षित है तो किस कक्षा तक _____

माँ – अशिक्षित /शिक्षित, अगर शिक्षित है तो किस कक्षा तक _____

भाई - बहन नाम अगर शिक्षित है तो किस कक्षा तक

भाई   बहन
1. _____   _____
2. _____   _____
3. _____   _____
4. _____   _____

Annexure 4 *Data on Violence*

Neha

- (Have you ever traveled out of Dakshinpuri?) 'Only when our parents take us. Not with friends.'
- 'Boys say things and pass on comments. That is why we don't like roaming around out here. My mother tells me to be back by 8 pm. However, my brother comes home at midnight. His job goes on till about 10–10:30. After that, he goes out with his friends. Our parents sometimes tell him; however, he does not listen.'
- 'I have seen fights taking place downstairs itself. I get scared. My mother tells me not to look. They fight very badly. Whenever there are cases of animosity, there have been incidents of stabbing as well.'
- 'When people see girls and boys roaming together, they have different thoughts in their minds. They can roam together, but some people think this and that.'
- 'Why will guys be scared? They walk very comfortably, without any heed. (The fights that take place among them..) those are fights to deal with their enmities… yes, I am scared of him… that if I end up having some animosity with him, then he might come and beat me too… but if someone does not have any animosity with anyone, they feel comfortable enough to walk about without any fear… sometimes when he comes late, we just hope that he has not gotten into a fight with anyone. So….'
- 'If there is a fight taking place in the house, they beat one another. For example, the husband beats his wife. No one goes to stop it. Even if one does, they end up getting beaten up. If the fight is taking place outside, people call the police. However, at home, neither do they call the police, nor does

anyone go to stop the fight. They say it is a family (personal) matter, and what could they even do about it.'

Nishant

- 'Earlier, crimes did not take place... now, there are crimes taking place in every other issue... earlier when there were fights, people used to hit each other with sticks, now there is a fight, there are gunshots and stabbing... (rate of crime is increasing because) some are because of the government... and some because of these movies... in south Indian movies they show action... people think that they will also do that to become famous... these movies have so many crimes... there was a boy named Ganju, very notorious... he used to roam around in all the streets... he had affiliations with a minister.'

- 'I am not scared (to stay here). See, my paternal uncle from Chirag Delhi has beaten up people, including Ganju. His son, who is now becoming a goon (*gunda*) touches his feet. The rest of the gang leaders from here also visit my uncle in Chirag Delhi, touch his feet. I have support... I have learned that from living here. Boys used to support boys. When one of the boys would pick a fight, the others used to come and back him up. From 8–10, I was in Sarvodaya, I used to be timid. After that, my father told me about my uncle. Since then, I have my force backing me. In class 11, whoever used to mess with me, even today I have been sitting in a position of power and domination over them. It is possible that they still know about my name and reputation in that school. Two of my brothers still attend that school (in Sarvodaya). The school authorities know they are Nishant's brothers. No one can antagonize or pick a fight with them.'

- 'Only Jat and Gujjar boys used to attend that school (in Sohna Road). I used to be the only one from Valmiki community. They used to roam around in groups and I was the only one from my community. You do know right how Jat, Gujjar people are? Shallow types. They used to lift girls' skirts up. One day, a guy lifted up my sister's friend's skirt. I beat that guy up. He then went out and called his guys… I also called my friends from Khanpur. My uncle made me meet a goon (*gunda*) from Deoli Village. He told me that I should contact him if I have any more problems in the future. He gave me his contact number.'

- 'They can study as long as they want to. 70 per cent girls go, 30 per cent don't. Because there has been no change in mindsets of people. This is why I joined this NGO. I bring my sister to all kinds of events. My father had told me that I could study as much as I wanted to. However, I have ensured that for my sister as well. Here, she has been able to enroll herself in the computer class. Our father has supported that. She will be now starting her basic course. Boys who start doing drugs mostly drop out after 10th standard.'

- 'You could call her as the smartest girl in her school. She used to not talk much to guys too. But, she was close to me. The other boys in the school were unhappy about her talking to me. See, we used to talk about the character (nature). Everything used to depend on that—who is she or will be talking to? Even here, I talk to everyone. I do not know whether I am or used to be attractive, but other people do tell that I have this attractive nature.'

- 'People laugh and mock at us saying that none of our family members drink or smoke while the rest of the locality does it. No one says it to our faces; they do not have the guts to do that. All the guys in the locality, including the ones who are older to me, respect me. They call me Sonu Bhai' (Masculinity and Caste—on the one hand he has shared about how the family attempts to hide their caste identity and on the other hand this almost boastful sharing of their comparative affluence within Dakshinpuri. Is it a sub-conscious way of compensating for the shame one feels regarding one part of their identity by displaying the other which one is proud of?)

- 'If a guy hits another guy, there is going to be a confronta-tion. Nowadays, it is not like that. When 4–5 guys stand together, one guy cannot do anything about it. He needs support. The guys that come to give support are ones that have already murdered someone. If anyone has that kind of support, that means that guy s very notorious. However, I am not like that. How much ever support the other person has, I do not back off from a fight. This is because I have my uncle's immense support, which I had mentioned to you earlier. That is why I am never scared. If someone harasses their sister, it is such that they are stabbed or beaten up by a bunch of guys. So I feel proud that no one tried to confront me. No one even tries to confront the other guys in the locality because they know this is Sonu's locality. The goons here respect and salute me.'

- 'The biggest kind of enmity arises when I talk to a girl and her brother's friend goes and complains to him. In this manner also, enmity arises. It does not matter if he is setting himself up with another girl; no one is allowed to talk to his sister. My sister and I have been going to a co-ed school since the beginning. People who go to government school have this kind of mindsets.'

- 'In the election, we are from UP. My father's hi-fi friends are from Delhi. The prayer ritual that we have for the pig, we just worship but do not consume the meat. In the village, people worship and then feed it to people in the village. I only eat the pudding (*halwa*). I stay away from these things. My great-grandfather used to do these prayer rituals. We have not made our prayer place here. Whenever we need to do any rituals, we go there. People stay there differently. We stay here, therefore we should have created our own place, but we did not.'
- 'There has been a Madrasi colony here from a very long time. My father had mentioned that they have been here since he was not married. I do not know where they have come from. They sell liquor at home. All of it is black money.'
- 'There are some people who live here and there. However, the Madrasi colony in Madangir is well known. They also live in 20, B block and D Block. The girls are scared that ever since the Madrasis have settled here, there are intoxicants available everywhere. Guys are often intoxicated. The day intoxication stops here, situation in Dakhinpuri will improve.' (Vishal, who is from Bihar, for example shared how the violence has increased here because of the Valimikis and their 'dirty' occupation of pig rearing. Nishant, a Valimiki blames it on the outsider Madrasis. While everyone has shared how the alcohol business here is run by a woman named Bobby who is a Madrasi.)

Rahul

- 'I do not go out alone; there is always someone with me. People drive their cars very rashly. People get scared and move to the side so that no one hits and runs over them.

I didn't know the roads very well and worried that I would be lost if I went here and there. Although I could not do it earlier, I am capable of it now. After 12th, I have started going to places by myself. I am still scared at night. In the daytime, I am confident to go anywhere. Even when a place is secluded, I get scared.'

- 'I am very scared of fights. I don't know why, but I am very scared of it. I get very nervous and my heart starts pounding hard (suddenly his voice changed). Whenever there is a fight anywhere, I try to stay as far from it as possible. It does not matter who is involved in it. In our home, no such fights take place. Brothers fight sometimes. If there is a fight in the locality or there is a huge fight, then I get scared. I get worried that I might get into a confrontation. I don't know what happens to me. I get tensed. I always tell myself that I will return only after the scuffle is over.'

- 'I am able to talk to the girls from here now. I never used to talk to them earlier. Now, when I have to ask them something, I do not hesitate to go ahead. Very few boys hesitate to talk to girls. Some of the girls talk to you when you engage in a conversation with them. There are some girls who do not respond. I have this fear from within. I engage in conversations with them very rarely. I get scared that I might end up saying something untoward. I just talk to the girls who stay near our house. I have not had any friends who are girls. I am the only one who does not talk to the girls; all the other guys do it. I have never had a friend who is a girl. I do not know how to engage in a conversation with them. There is a sense of fear in approaching them. I will not even go anywhere where a girl is standing. I get worried that someone might ask me where I am going; the girls living in the first floor might ask. Then I decided that if someone asks,

I will tell them that there is a meeting upstairs where I have been called. However, if I have left from here, then I do not go upstairs. I have not talked (to the girls who have come here). If they have asked something, I have responded; that is all I have talked.'

Rajesh

- 'Yes, I am still very scared since my brother stays out till midnight–1 am. So I get worried. After the clock strikes 10 pm, we call him after every 15 minutes. There are a lot of people who are intoxicated at that hour, so we get scared. Our father has advised that even if someone says a thing or two, listen to it and come back and to not retaliate or respond.' (Fear for the boys of the family—a recurrent theme and the strategy used to save oneself is restriction in mobility but only post sunset.)
- 'My brother was once stopped by a police officer near Khanpur. I called our uncle immediately. He instantly went on his bike there and showed his NDMC card. However, the police officer did not let go of my brother. Uncle then called his brother who works in the PM house. On seeing his card, the police officer let him go. He returned home around 4 am. He had shown his identity card, but the police officer had not allowed him to leave. Only later he was allowed to leave. Father has grown up and is used to the lifestyle in the village. He walked all the way to Khanpur in his casual clothes.'
- '(Girls are scared) but it's not like they do not come. There are four–five airhostesses who come back from work at 3–4 am. However, there is pressure from the family to not go out. There is a set mentality that one should not go out after

10 pm as the surroundings are not safe at that time. Our sister also comes and goes out at night. So many people go to and come back from call centers. People who travel up and down everyday know about it. Yes, if they go to some other places, then it is scary.'

- 'One day, I had bunked my classes and went to visit India Gate. I had seen it for the first time then. It was then that I did everything. I had gone to see Akshardham as well. The school had once taken us to Nainital that was my first time there. All of my friends had gone with me.'

Roshan

- 'If they roam around, there will be no conversations; the guy will end up getting beaten up. Couples (girlfriend and boyfriend) never meet up in their own locality. It is very rarely that they meet up in their own area. They meet us secretly; far away from the localities that they live in.'

- 'Looting takes place a lot. Snatching happens to a great extent. Money is snatched by stabbing people. There are a lot of cases of murders. People are not in their sound mind after drinking excessively. They just need to beat someone else up. Intoxication is one of the biggest reasons for this. Whatever the substance of intoxication is… Wherever there is intoxication, there is violence.'

- 'I get scared. These incidents take place in the night or when there is old animosity among people. I get scared and I go out alone… I have money in my pocket. I always check my surroundings to see if there is anything I can hit with… anything on the ground that I can defend myself with. This is all I can do. While guys are scared that they will be driven away by the police or that they don't get beaten up, girls are worried that they do not get harassed at night. For everyone, there is the fear of being looted and having their belongings snatched. While the guys are scared of pocket shears or rods that someone might take out in case of a fight, girls are scared of being harassed at night. That is why they do not leave their houses after 10 pm.'

- 'Yesterday itself, I had seen a man beat up his wife. I did not say anything. I do not know them. They say it is their personal matter… and even if a girl says this, then one or two will go to help, but will also rebuke about it. That is why no one goes. The next day they are casually asked if they are doing okay. These issues are solved among themselves. If not, the police are there, Mahila Panchayat is there. I have not seen the case proceedings in a Mahila Panchayat, but I have seen hearings take place. ASHA workers are present there. Every member of the family is questioned. They are explained and then asked what they want. Decisions are made after that based on that. If it is absolved then, it is okay, otherwise the case is proceeded to the district court. Panchayat Head, Sarpanch or a lawyer makes the final decisions after discussing it with their peers.'

Roshani

- 'Knives and machetes… these are easily found in the market. These were earlier done by older people. Now, even the children do it. In the slum areas, both the parents work. Nowadays, all the women work to meet the needs of the family. Therefore, there is no one at home to take care of the children.'
- 'In the government school, when a group comes together, they usually know things about one another. Everyone is

together. In the school, even a minute thing becomes huge. There is peer pressure and support that if my friend has done this, I can do it too. Children drop out in groups of 2–3. Two others had dropped out when my cousin had dropped out of school. They earn by doing small tasks and fulfil their needs with that money. Children are ready to work even for meager amounts of money. With that money, they get to do whatever they want.'

- 'I am definitely scared. Not extremely scared, but yes, I get worried that my family does not fall prey to this. Whoever it is, be it my younger sister, it does affect us. She is young, so we need to look out for her, the kind of friends she is making, whom we should ask her to stay away from.'

- 'The innocent and naive guys are scared. If a guy is naive and does not say much because of his family, he is taken advantage of. However, if a guy is frank and has lots of friends around him, then he is fine. Innocent guys are made fun of by other guys. There have been so many instances where weak guys are baited into trouble. The police are given money and they are put in trouble.'

- 'With Taaj, I go just about everywhere. She was working, so she used to get free from work at 5 pm and then we used to go to eat *samosas* together. While eating *samosas*, we used to reach south Indian. Even if we did not want to actually go shopping, we used to go to the market to do window shopping. We used to roam around in Dakshinpuri and in the parks, we avoid Sanjay Camp. We used to go back home by 8 pm. Three of us (Taaj, Roshani and Muskaan) used to get scolded every day. Once we got busy, we used to find it difficult to give time to friends. Now, we mostly speak over the phone. Sometimes our conversations go on for so long that mother asks who I am talking to.'

- 'My classes used to take place every Sunday in Hansraj College. Because of the long distance between home and college, my brother did not allow me to go. My brother and mother asked why I am going to college since no studies happen. I told them that classes do take place, however, they still did not allow me to go.'

Sara

- 'Husband hits his wife.... Tell me, how else will anyone stand up against the husband when the wife herself stands by him? Look at Naziya only.... It is the same case. She used to be my best friend. She used to share everything with me. Now in her marriage, such a big issue happened; she did not even tell me about it.'
- 'I do not go out of the house after 10 pm. My aunt (paternal) and I go out together. Earlier we used to hear from people or read in the newspapers about murders taking place here. Now, there are murders taking place in Dakshinpuri. Guys keep guns as well. The atmosphere here has been deteriorating with each passing day. We become what our surroundings need us to be. Very small children smoke cigarettes and hookah, and what else… they get intoxicated. The goons (*gundas*) here are not very well educated. The only thing in their minds is how to earn more money, how they can show off, how to be famous… they put up videos on Youtube… if they can make a video of a murder taking place, they can also stop the murder from taking place. No one is willing to come forward and help.'
- 'Everyone in the house is busy doing their jobs… everyone is busy trying to make money. Both the husband and wife go for work. No one pays attention to the children. They roam around idly. They do not get any guidance from

their parents. Those who send their children to government schools, they never go to the schools to check if their children are attending their classes and studying. They never check their textbooks and notebooks.'

- 'If I become something big, then I will leave. So many murders take place here. My father also drinks and I get so worried about him lying drunk somewhere. I just hope no one finds him or how much money he has in his pockets. Guys come and snatch away the money. Even until uncle comes back home, we keep waiting outside for him to reach home. He is a chef. A cab comes to drop him off, still... I will look after myself by not leaving the house, but I get worried for the others.'

- 'Guys are disgusting... They pass comment... if I say something in return, they get angry. I feel like beating them up... but they stay in groups, so can't even think about it. Maybe today I am not alone, but tomorrow, if I am traveling alone, they might come and hit/beat me. That is why I keep quiet. When I was younger, I used to hit and my parents used to receive complaints about it. I used to roam around earlier so much that I was told that I should stay home. Only if I have some work, I should go out. Even though I am grown up, my father still does not allow me to go out. Nowadays I only don't feel like going out as I feel unsafe when I am outside.'

- 'I used to pray that Allah makes me a boy in my next life. Being a girl, I am not happy. Anywhere I go, I feel unsafe. I feel weird that I have to take permission for one thing or another. (If I am a guy) I will be able to make my own decisions... I will not have to wash utensils. Although it is claimed that we are treated equally in our home, actions show the gendered division. All the brothers wear jeans and no one has ever questioned their choice to wear jeans. That question never arises with them. However, if I put on a pair of jeans, I am questioned for my choice. My cousin and I wear jeans, no one else. They even say that girls who use phone before they get married are spoiled. I have told them that whoever wants to really use a phone, will find ways to use, for example, from friends. I keep my phone locked at all times. You never know when my father will want to use it!'

Shahana

- 'When my father had arrived here, he was a goon (*gunda*) too. He was such that if he saw a girl with a guy, he would beat up the guy and take the girl back to her house. Earlier, wearing jeans was not allowed here. Even father did not like it at all. Whenever he saw someone's sister wearing jeans, a group consisting of my father, uncle and others would go to the girl's house and complain to her parents. And they had quite an influence among the people there. Ever since all of them got married, the group has now become scattered. They have stopped doing a lot of things. Earlier, my father used to drink, not anymore. My mother has had a good influence on him.'
- 'My brother does not have friends from this locality; all of them are from outside of this locality. He is friends with many influential people. All the boys hang out beside the Mosque on their bikes. There are a minimum of 50 bikes parked there where they hang out. My brother plays there, so he meets them there. Because he is small in stature, everyone keeps hitting him. We ask him all the time if someone has hit him and threatened him to not talk about it at home. He always responds in the negative. Children from outside tell us what happens in reality.'

- 'Sanjay Camp has completely changed from what it was earlier. Action India has worked intensively there. Earlier it was like this. Mother used to have meetings there. The place has changed quite a lot and all the credit goes to Action India. Otherwise, I never used to talk this much. I have learned to talk openly after joining Action India. Now my sister tells me that I talk so much, I don't know how to stop. Whenever we call the boys for a meeting, they show up. However, when we call the fathers for a meeting, they do not show up. Therefore, they do not have the awareness and understanding about how to solve different problems. The women who stay at home come for these meetings and become aware of such issues.'

- 'No, I don't think so. No one ever harasses me. They are very scared of me. I just look at them and they keep shut. My sister asks me to ignore if someone catcalls or says anything. How much will I ignore it? One day it will cross my limit. The other day, I was returning from somewhere when one guy called me out by saying I look very nice. I responded saying that he did not look nice at all. My sister asked why I had to respond to such things. I told her that I did not like anyone passing such comments and on top of that, me having to keep quiet about it. If I respond with a thank you, he will try to carry the conversation forward and I do not like that.'

- 'I do not go anywhere. I only got to Roshani's place or she comes to visit me. Taaj comes over sometimes. Exams are going on at the moment, so we do not go out anywhere. Otherwise, on other days, my sister, Roshani, Taaj and I go out to the park. The park is huge. There are three roads leading to the park. We really enjoy it there.'

- 'We are scared of our brother. One is our brother, another is our father. This is because our father used to be very short tempered earlier. He used to get into a lot of fights. When our mother was there, he was not scared of anyone. Ever since she is not here anymore, he has calmed down understanding that if he keeps getting involved in fights, there will be no one to look after his children as there is no other support system to look after them. Therefore, he now goes to the extent of joining his hands, pleading and solving his issues.'

- 'I go to the market. Lajpat Nagar, Sarojini Nagar... and Madangir market here... there is a need to go to the market almost every day to buy household essentials and vegetables.'

- 'Everyone does not tell the truth and go out. They never get caught. I inform the truth at home that I am going to the park because my father drives the e-rickshaw on this road; therefore he will know if I am lying. Therefore, I inform and go out. Roshani also informs at home. However, Taaj has some issues at home. On Sundays, she tells them she is going to the park, but on weekdays she comes here by telling them at home that she is going out for her tuitions. She never gets caught though. She never tells her mother because her mother gets extremely worried. If people get caught here, they get beaten up. What else?'

- 'This is because the atmosphere here is very spoiled. Fights break out even in the smallest of cases of conflicts. Big guys beat up younger guys. They make them work, demand for money to be sent. That is why I had mentioned earlier that we get more worried for our brother. I am not at all scared to live here. The older guys bully the younger ones to do all kinds of work. "Go to my home, get this thing." (He gets paid to do such things.) I don't know... he never tells us about anything that happens to him. Even when he has gotten beaten up, he does not come home and tell us about it.'

- 'My brother comes back from school at 2 pm after which he watches television for an hour. He then goes out. If I am home then I look for him and bring him back home. After that, he runs away again when I go out for my tuition. On the way back from my tuition, I get hold of him once again and bring him back home and make him sit next to me. I tell him that watch TV if you want, but do not go out. He has gotten very spoiled by going outside. Because of him, people from outside come to fight with us saying your brother has been doing this, he has been doing that even when he has sometimes not done anything. People may also be lying. We really need to keep him in control. We are planning on now sending him to the hostel. He has really gotten spoiled. He roams around a lot and does not even study. My sisters are not home during the day and he does not listen to me. He has been getting low marks in his classes. Our father also leaves for work in the morning and comes back home at night. When father is home, he is also home. Father does not beat him, just scolds him; but he pays no attention to that. We do not beat him, he is our only brother. Sometimes when my anger threshold is crossed, I hit him though. At that point, I hit him with whatever I have in my hand, be it a rolling pin or tongs. I have beaten him when he was younger too. I was very rude. That has never gotten me into any kind of trouble though. I have never given any outsider a chance to say that your girl is doing this.'
- 'When we were younger, our mother was there to control us. I used to be very scared of her. However, she never allowed anyone to hit him. Earlier, our father used to hit him because he was very naughty. Mother used to get very

angry then, she used to not eat her food and make our father promise her that he will not raise his hands again on him. She used to always say "I have only one son... I have only one son." This has gotten into his head that since he is the only son, no one will raise a hand on him. This is why he has gotten more spoiled. While he is a little scared of our elder sister, he does not listen to our father at all. He will behave himself for an hour or so and he will be back in his old ways again. He is scared of our elder sister since she is older and also raises hands on him... but he knows me. He is scared of her only. There is no one now to control him that much. In our times, with the ones we used to be scared of, we also used to fear that they will hit us. This does not apply for him.'

• 'Why will boys be scared? They always keep roaming about outside. Who will they be scared of? My brother is indifferent to the consequences of his actions. I am older; therefore I understand the consequences of his actions. He enjoys roaming around outside, to stay here and to talk to other boys. I know how wrong his actions are. No one is scared. All of them keep roaming around outside.'

Shiksha

• 'When my father comes back from the market, he always sees the big group standing there. That is why he asks me not to go out. I am also not allowed to go out at night. At night, you will not see any girls outside, only guys.'

• 'What will boys be scared of? Some guys think that because a lot of guys here threaten and bully; however, all guys are not like that. Some are nice and innocent. Maybe they are scared of staying here. People who shift to Dakhinpuri from outside, they find it difficult to adjust at first. However, over time, they also get used to it.'

Taaj

- 'We go to South Indian (a restaurant in Madangiri). I go to the park after my tuition… on Sundays, to Sarojini Market. We make a group, take an auto or book a cab and go there. I tell the people at home that there are four of us going out. We also go to Green Park, Saket mall with friends… We go to CP also in a group.'

- 'No, no, they do not know at home that I have guy friends. They know that I work there, but they do not know that I have guy friends there. I just know them and interact with them at work… they know it like that. I do not talk to them once I am home. We work together, so we get to know each other. There was an instance once… I was once standing next to a railing in the office and talking to Faizan *bhaiya* (computer teacher in AI) and another guy… my aunt's son, who is a driver, was there just downstairs… he saw me talking to them… he told my family that I keep talking to guys. I had told him that I work there… and that I was discussing about mobilization. I work, so I talk about work. I became adamant. Even if you are standing next to your brother and interacting, they say that I keep talking to guys. Even if the guy you talk to a guy who is a friend, then they say that she keeps roaming around with guys. This is why we meet up in South Indian… eat and drink there comfortably. I have a cousin (maternal uncle's son) with whom I share everything. He is my best friend… best bro, just like Rohit. Even if I go here or there, I share that information with him. My family does not know that I am this close to him. They do not like that. Once, there was this incident; I had gone with my cousin Bunty on his bike to go buy a shirt for him in Madangir as it was his birthday. My mother had told me then that she understands he is my brother, but people still talk among themselves about these things.'

- (Is forced marriage a common thing?) 'Yes, it happens like that only out here. The husband thinks of his wife as his property. This is how it happens only after marriage. Even if there is a discussion regarding dowry or any other thing, then they beat the wife up... they don't do anything... just keep sitting silently at home... I had reached out to one woman and had informed her about Mahila Panchayat. She had gone there, but then she went back home and the same thing continued. We inform them about the Mahila Panchayats through our Disha program. A lot of people came asking for help, they were offered help as well. (why is it that) these people are illiterate... people who indulge in intoxication... beat up for the smallest of reasons... start fights over small things... all young children do it... these things happen a lot.'

- 'When someone tried to tell me anything, I give it off to them. If they tell me one thing, I tell them two other things... can't stand it. If someone tells me anything, I get very angry. One day, one guy from our locality was saying something and I responded saying, I told one, "Do I look like I belong to your father?... don't you know what organization I work for? I can file a complaint about you harassing me." His mother then told me to go to her if her son does something like that again. You can't stay quiet here. They will say one thing, if you do not respond, they will say another thing. Therefore, I respond in the first go itself.

Other girls blush and smile in the first time and then the guys continue to harass them.'
- 'Guys are not scared of anything. They stay fearlessly. What problem do they face? Because they are boys, they have this freedom since they are young. Even if they roam around late at night, what have they got to fear? Mothers also side with their sons. Even if they are up to something, the mothers defend them by saying that whatever their sons are doing, at least their daughter are not doing anything wrong.'

Tina

- 'No, what do guys have to fear about? It is not like girls are harassing them here. All the boys here are goons. They understand that no one can speak to them in response if they say thing. On top of that, their family members let them do whatever they want, whenever they want to come home, they go out anytime, they are not stopped. Parents think what will the boys do by studying.. How much ever you hit them, they do not listen. It does not matter. Therefore, they see no point in scolding the boys.'
- 'Boys and girls talk a lot here. I have never seen anyone not being able to talk. I think that till today, I have hardly talked like that to anyone ever, or with any boy. It is not allowed to talk so much in our house even with brothers.'
- (What do you do when someone comments) 'Nothing. I do not even dare to look. I keep my gaze down and walk away. When Jyoti asks if I saw or heard the comment, I say no, I did not see anyone. I always hope we do not end up in a scuffle when Jyoti responds to such comments. That's why I ask her to stay silent and not respond or say anything to anyone.'

- 'Fights do happen here in people's homes... between husband and wife. The husband often comes home drunk and beats up his wife unnecessarily. If the wife is working, the husband demands her to give him money for his alcohol. Some people try and stop the fights telling the husband not to beat up, saying that she does not have any fault. Our locality is useless. There is a fight going on and people are laughing on the streets about it. They are just jealous thinking how come they have a job, or how come their children are doing so well. They are jealous of one another.'

Vishal

- 'People get into a fight even if a small thing happens. Like if there is a fight between siblings in the house, they also come out in the park and quarrel. The people from the neighborhood never used to get involved earlier, now they also join in, saying that how dare your sister tell you like this. The problem is with children nowadays, they do not understand. It is the parents' fault that they do not guide their children correctly. If you guide well, the atmosphere will not deteriorate. Children more than adults....'
- 'Mother feels that way. If I leave the house after 8 at night and my father's friends see me, they scold me for roaming around late at night.'
- 'On holidays, I leave Dakshinpuri in the morning and come back only in the evening. Ansal Plaza, Faridabad, mall... garden.'
- 'If guys are not safe here, what do you think will happen to girls? When a girl enters Dakshinpuri, she either calls her parents or friends. They then come to escort her home. Restrictions are placed on her, she is not allowed to leave

the house, and she has to leave her job. There is a fear for the girl that if someone sees her talking to a guy, even as a brother, her parents will be informed. They will tell her brother who will then beat her, stop her from leaving the house, go to school and tuition. She will have to stop talking to everyone.'

- 'Until you step out of the house, you will not fear anything. Earlier, I too did not leave the house much. Till I was in school, my father used to scare me that someone will come take me away, so I was afraid to go out. I was afraid to even go down the stairs. Then after the 12th exam, when I was waiting for the result... In those two months I went out a lot... went around with everyone, everyone started to get to know me. Till you do not leave the house and unless you learn to distinguish the good and the bad, you will be scared.'

- 'Even boys have the worry that no one should find out that he is talking to a girl, even if he considers her a sister. Parents will ask why I am talking to her. When I tell them, they will still understand; it is the outsiders who have an opinion and will tell them that 'no, she is his girlfriend'. The boy does not face too many repercussions. He will not be allowed to leave the house for a day or two, and then the issue will be solved. It is the girl who has to face severe consequences.'

- 'When my father came here, he was a well-built man. Sunny and Bobby were his friends. Everyone called him Jeetu *Bhai*. I had once accompanied my father to Bobby's 36th birthday. All the goons had come... Sunny, Kunal, Sneh ... Everyone asked if I am Jeetu *Bhai*'s son... I call everyone as uncle. On my way back home, I found uncle on the way and he dropped me off home on his bike. 15 other people had come along in their bikes to drop me. Everyone around was watching that.'

- 'When we were young, our grandmother's health had become very bad. So, father sent my mother and me to the village to be with her. He was then living here alone. He used to have the freedom to be with his friends then. He did not drink and all, but he used to spend a lot of time with his friends. He then got into a fight with one of his friends. But there is a great difference between the fights that used to take place earlier and now. Earlier there was a compromise, it does not happen nowadays. Now, people are just finished off.'

Manisha

- 'I don't go out that much. Even if I do, it is just in our own street. Our locality is alright. There are not many fights taking place or anything. If anything happens in the locality, we are not allowed to go out. If someone has to go out to buy anything, he, mother or my father goes out to get it. We three don't go anywhere. We only go to visit our grandparents… or to the mall. We party when we go to our friends' places—Christmas party, New Year Party… If we want to go to the mall, we go with our brother.'
- 'My mother does not refuse though… if I take my elder brother with me. If all girls are there, then I go out with them only, not too far though. It is difficult because the aunties around here keep observing you. Even if I talk a little, they will go and tell my family. That is why my mother tells me not to talk much with anyone. I go shopping with my mom. I shop online as well. There will be sale on the online platforms during Diwali. I buy things from Amazon. I use Big Basket to buy vegetables.'
- 'I feel very scared. Even when I was coming here, I walked briskly looking nowhere else. I don't like going out

alone. That is why my father also does not allow me to go alone very far. I do not speak to anyone. Even if someone passes a comment, I look straight and walk off. My mother has advised me to not respond to anyone and to call if there is a serious problem.'

- 'Yes, there are fights at homes. However, if the fights are severe, they go to the Mahila Panchayat. They help with divorces as well. My mother also regularly goes to the Mahila Panchayat, so she knows a lot. She helps if any incidents take place in the locality.'

- 'Sometimes I get very frustrated that just the moment I step out of the house, my parents receive a call from someone.'

- 'Everyone at home knows about my Facebook account. My elder brother has my password as well. He accesses it and checks once in a while. He was the one that has created the account for me. Everyone goes with my cousin. There is no problem. Even if someone sees it on Facebook, there is no issue. I do not have such things. He checks my phone as well; there is no problem there as well. Sometimes I get very angry that he keeps checking my phone but he does not show me his phone and what's in it. But what to do? It's okay. If I say something, he will hit me.'

- 'He does not have to be scared of anything. He roams around with confidence. He is not afraid of anyone, not even the police. He passes comments and calls out people on the streets with no fear of anyone. This is why I do not like the guys here. He does not go out much. He goes to college or for tuitions. He goes to our elder sister's place. He does not stay here much.'

- 'Some girls are not able to talk much. They are extremely scared to talk to anyone because, in Dakshinpuri, everyone knows one another. If a girl talks to a guy, someone or the other will tell her parents. My mother has told me that if I talk to any guy, whether it is a friend or a brother. Someone will definitely come to tell my family at home. This is why girls are scared to talk. That is why girls talk to their guy friends in tuition and all, but not on the streets.'

• 'If I go somewhere, I don't always tell the truth of where I am going to my mother. I don't tell them if I get harassed anywhere. If I tell her, I think she will blame me only.'

Akshay

• 'If I get angry for some reason at home, I cannot express it or take it out on anyone at home. I go out and take it out by beating up someone outside and breaking their bones. Be innocent at home and notorious outside. I hang out with the Jats from Gurgaon. Their lifestyle is very different. You must be having friends from here; you may know their ways. I really enjoy hanging out with them. We drive around at 2–3 am and there is no one to stop us. If the police stop us, we just put him on a call with one of the MLAs they know and the issue gets solved. In Delhi, I need to act very innocent… (in school) I have made such friends that I have been involved in theft with them. I became like the friends I had made. The person that we had beaten up, we had taken away his money as well. We used to get the money and spend it to eat at a hotel. We used to eat well with 50 rupees. My friends used to have money. Whenever someone had a birthday, they used to distribute toffees in the class. When they used to come to give us, we used to throw the toffees on their faces, telling them that toffees don't fill our stomachs, and to treat us in a hotel instead. We used to take them and spend their 100 rupees on ourselves. We used to do all that.'

• 'I can bring 10 guys from Dakshinpuri and make them stand here this very moment. This is how the environment is. Within seconds, there will be a gun out. I am not scared. I have seen a murder take place when I was a child. I have seen a lot of murders take place. I do not fear anyone. Like how it happens among brothers... my father had once beaten my mother and injured her head, when the police came, they did nothing. When my brother beat up my dad and injured his head, then also the police did nothing. Now I am very used to these things. Now I have toughened myself enough to not be affected by anything.'

• 'We had beaten up a guy from the mosque. He then brought all the guys from the mosque. We brought different things from the ironsmith and beat them up. The police had come too, but then everything was over by then. I have never let my name come on the radar of the police. And now, many of them know me so well that they greet me and ask how I am doing.'

• 'If the girl does not stay well, someone will take her away/pick her up. If she has made a boyfriend, she is safe. If she is married, she is safe. The girls who keep roaming here and there in the name of tuitions, it won't take very long for them to be harassed. The ones who say they go for tuitions, I know all their stories. There are no innocent people here in Dakshinpuri. The moment a girl steps out of her house, she meets 30 guys. Why will girls be scared? They have Mahila Panchayats. The police take strict action. If you tell one of the *bhaiyas* that this person has behaved in this manner, the guy will be beaten up immediately. Then you

are on your own. You can easily dial 100 (helpline). The
Mahila Panchayat has made it very convenient. How are
girls not safe then? If they are on their own, then what?'

- 'Why do murders take place here? You can pay someone to
have them murdered. You need to kidnap any girl; you just
pay someone to do it. No girl can however get a guy kid-
napped. You need guts to do things like these. If you ask a
guy to get something done, he will also want something in
return. No one takes such a big gamble. You get it right?
There will be problems.'

- 'Everyone says Akshay *Bhai*, we do not want to fight with
you. Everyone calls me "brother" and gives me respect. If I
get into a fight, then my brother settles and puts an end to it.
My brother hangs out with the politicians. My brother is good
in studies as well as in hooliganism. Guys ask me how I have
so much money. I say that gamble. Place bets, do anything,
but you should know how to earn money.'

Ankita

- 'It is regular. They say it is a natural thing now. Earlier when
it used to happen, I used to get scared. Now, no one is
scared. Just some time ago, someone had beaten another
person up. This is a very regular thing now. There are a lot
of animosities. There were two friends and one of them got
in a relationship with the other's sister, then a fight broke
out as to how he dared to do that. One of them had picked
up an axe to hit the other. What is this? He should be happy
that his friend is in a relationship with his sister, and that
he at least knows him well. When a guy gets into a relationship with another guy's sister, then he doesn't think that is
wrong. I don't have a mindset like this.'

- 'I hit my brother a lot. I don't allow him to go out. I make him understand by citing him various examples.'
- 'If it is 9 pm, the girl will not go out whatsoever and however important the need is to go out. I do not go out anywhere. I do not go out with my friends as well. Sometimes I don't go to meet ups; sometimes I am not allowed to go. I am not allowed to go out much. If there is some public meeting or if I want to explore any place, I am not allowed to go there. I do not know how to travel on my own. I do not know how to go to these far off places like Dwarka. That is why I quit. I am not very scared, but yeah, there is a fear that I might get lost.'

Daalchand

- 'Earlier, this place was not that scary. Now there is bloodshed, the crimes have increased. Earlier, everyone used to support each other. Now, many come here drunk... Many do not work, they sit at home and keep fighting... on each other. Earlier, the neighbors used to say that "why are you making a stir, solve it at home." Now they directly complain to the police... The police also help solve the problem for a while... Both sides will then be taken to the police station. These issues are never sorted out... This area is considered as bad and that the people belonging here are bad... people here start considering themselves as notorious. So why don't we do bad things? If we are being falsely accused, why should we not do the same thing? If they are accusing you of smoking cigarettes, then it does become a bad habit. If you have a bad name already, what is the harm in working? People start acquiring bad habits once that is internalized. Children start fighting, locally made weapons become easily available and people start hitting with whatever they have in hand, including pencils, stones etc.'

- 'Now, I am not scared anymore. You get used to it when you have lived here. The only issue is people at random come here to fight. For example, if someone is riding his bike in a very rash manner, they will blame you for coming onto the street. If someone does not respond and quietly move away, they will target another person. If someone retaliates, they will pick a fight with them. Parents get worried that children should not leave the house after 8–9 pm... that they should be in their locality only. If an innocent friend of yours get beaten up, it then becomes your responsibility that you friend got beaten up in front of your house. That is why, if there is anything, it is exchanged through a phone call or it is taken care of the next morning. This place becomes a tense environment at night.'

- (How do you keep yourself safe?) '... By not going into a place where there is a crowd... by going from the side... so that no one gets a chance to say anything... Never go out alone. If there is a fight taking place, people come to join in... after that I don't know... although outside I show like I am not afraid, inside there is a fear. It might not be my fault, but I don't know how others will react....'

- 'Everyone is scared. For girls, it is that they are not able to talk. A guy might not understand it. Girls are allowed to go to school and tuitions and then go back home. They cannot roam around outside. If they are able to continue with their studies till college, they become much more unreserved. They learn to travel on their own. Those who are not able to reach college, they stay at home only. At the max, they are allowed to go visit their relatives. They cannot roam around like how guys roam around. They might go out on a weekend. Now, the environment here has become bad. If someone is seen going out alone, it is assumed that they are going out to meet another person. They think that without a doubt that they are going to do something wrong. Girls are also scared of getting harassed and catcalled out here. There are some guys who are always looking for some kinds of opportunities, even if they are with anyone, including their family. The family members start assuming that the girl knows the guy because why would a stranger otherwise speak to her. There is suspicion placed on the girl. If the family is more understanding, they ask her for the truth; if not, they start having suspicion on her. As a result, she ends up getting married off early or made to drop out from school and continue with open schooling.'

Jyoti

- 'People pass comments on boys and girls. Uncle-aunties keep staring. People look with a bad gaze. They start gossiping that this person was here, found there... Boyfriend-girlfriend roams around indifferently as they do not care about anything else. They ignore whatever falls on their ears. If they are caught, they are not allowed to go out of the house. If they get caught a second time, they are not allowed to go to school... they are not allowed to go out on the street. This only happens to girls. This does not happen for boys because they do not listen. Girls on the other hand get beaten up!'
- 'In Sanjay Camp, I am scared. When I once went there at night, there were only guys outside. "Meet me outside"... that is how they say. Some of them do drugs; smoke cigarettes... parents say that.'

- 'I feel that my brother is not scared. The environment here is such that we get worried. We have only one brother. He is not allowed to go out much. He does not go out at night, but he is always out during the day. He does not listen to us. He does not listen to our father as well. Sometimes, he is scolded and made to stay inside.'
- 'Earlier, I used to be scared, not anymore. Now I respond when someone says something. I am scared of some people though… who are huge… those who are drunk… I am scared of those people. Otherwise, it is very normal for me now. I see groups of guys in every corner of the street. Now I inform at home also, earlier I never used to. My sister also informs, even my friends inform their families. Everyone's friends come over… so now I inform my family.'
- 'Nowadays, girls roam around. Some even stay at home. Some have curfews and they are allowed to stay out only till a certain time, like 8 or 9 pm I keeping sitting outside with my sister and aunt till 11 pm. We watch videos on the phone… chat and laugh around.'
- 'I think guys may be scared. For example, there are fights that take place among friends, murders… someone gets into a fight with another, someone goes away at night… these things keep happening.'

Kabir

- 'This whole area is not good. Section 144 has been imposed here. If a guy is seen outside after 10 pm, he is beaten up. Section 144 has been imposed because a murder had taken place here some time ago. It had taken place inside the police station. Some police officers have even been suspended. Now they have become very strict at night.'

- 'People from the other block come and do things here. If they say sorry, no fights take place.'
- 'I do not go out much… I just go for my tuition and then come back home. If I want to go out, I go out elsewhere. After 10 pm, my mother does not allow me to go out. Do whatever you want, but at home. My mother gets very worried because she knows that the whole area gets sealed, so she worries that I might also get picked up someday. Ever since 3–4 cases have taken place here, she tells me even more now not to go out. In the daytime, she never says anything. Earlier, I was allowed to go out at night, not anymore. More cases happen like this, because the police have imposed it here.'
- 'No, fights keep taking place. There are a lot of men here who get drunk and beat up their wives. Neighbors sometimes save them as well. If the son is old enough, he helps; if he is still young, he gets beaten up or goes out of the house. People from the locality try to stop them. They grab the man and take him away.'
- 'No, girls are not scared since they do not go out of the house much. Even if they go out, they do so in the day time. They come back home by 8–8:30 pm. At this hour, people are awake and outside. Nothing can happen at that time. After that, there are less people outside. After that hour if they want to go out, they get accompanied by an older sister, aunt etc… otherwise, they are not allowed to go out anyway. They have to stay home and even if they go out, they will be accompanied by someone. When they are younger, they are allowed to go out. Once they become older, there are more restrictions. My mother says that it is useless for girls to go out… they get picked up by guys, they do bad things to the

girls, plan to make videos of them. This is why people do not allow girls to go out, especially unaccompanied. They are often allowed to go out with an uncle or someone.'

- 'My sister only goes out when she has her friends with her. Otherwise, she just stays in our locality or at home. She goes out only with her friends or with someone older from the family. Yes, our mother goes out. She is old. No one can tell her anything. She will not spare anyone if someone says something.'

Bibliography

Adolescents in India: A Desk Review of Existing Evidence and Behaviours, Programmes and Policies. (2013). New Delhi: Population Council And UNICEF.

AICAR Business School (2015, 30 March). 'Economics for Everyone: Demographic Dividend'. *IndiaInfoOnline*. Available at: https://www.indiainfoline.com/article/print/news-top-story/economics-for-everyone-demographic-dividend-115033000296_1.html

Baxi, U. (Ed). (1988). Law and Poverty: Critical Essays. Bombay: N. M. Tripathi, viii.

Bhan, G. (2016). *In the Public's Interest, Evictions, Citizenship and Inequality in Contemporary India*. Hyderabad, New Delhi: Orient BlackSwan Private Limited.

Booth, A. & Hess, E. (1974). 'Cross-Sex Friendship'. *Journal of Marriage and Family*, 36: 138–47.

Chakraborty, K. (2009). '"The Good Muslim Girl": Conducting Qualitative Participatory Research to Understand the Lives of Young Muslim Women in the *Bustees* of Kolkata'. *Children's Geographies*, 7: 4, 421–34.

Chakraborty, K. (2016). 'Eve Teasing and Education Mobility: Young Women's Experiences in the Urban Slums of India'. GYCP Book Series, Volume 4. Singapore: Springer Science + Business Media, 1–16.

Chakraborty, K. (2014) 'Young People's Mobile Phone Culture in the Urban Slums of Kolkata'. In N. C. Schneider & F. M. Titzmann (eds), *Studying Youth, Media and Gender in Post-liberalisation India - Focus on and Beyond the 'Delhi Gang Rape'*. Berlin: Frank & Timme GmBh., 191–214.

Chakraborty, K. (2010). 'Unmarried Muslim Youth and Sex Education in the *Bustees* of Kolkata'. *South Asian history and Culture*, Volume 1, 2010 - Issue 2: Health, Culture and Religion: Critical Perspectives: edited by Assa Doron and Alex Broom, 268–81.

Ciotti, M. (2006). 'In the Past We Were a Bit "Chamar": Education as a Self and Community Engineering'. *Journal of the Royal Anthropological Institute* (N.S.), 899–916.

Das, V. (1989). 'Voices of Children'. *Daedalus*, 118: 262–94.

Dasgupta, C. (2001). 'Youth Gangs and Violence–Subordinated Adolescents' Road to Alternative Masculinity'. Psychological Foundations (Issue theme: Violence), 25–29.

Davis, K. (1941). 'Intermarriage in Caste Societies'. *American Anthropologist*, New Series, Vol. 43, No. 3, Part 1 (Jul.–Sep., 1941), 376–95.

Dugger, Celia (1998, 12 October). 'India's Hottest Political Issue: The Price of Onions'. *New York Times*. Available at: https://www.nytimes.com/1998/10/12/world/india-s-hottest-political-issue-the-price-of-onions.html

Edley, N. (2017). *Men and Masculinity: The Basics*. UK: Routledge.

Engels, F. (1902). The Origin of the Family, Private Property and the State. Available at: https://www.gutenberg.org/files/33111/33111-h/33111-h.htm

Eve, M. (2002). 'Is Friendship a Sociological Topic?' *European Journal of Sociology* 43: 3, 386–409.

Gill, R. (2007). *Gender and Media*. Cambridge: Polity Press.

Gunnarsson, L. (2015). 'Loving Him for Who He is: The Microsociology of Power'. In A. G. Jonasdottir & A. Ferguson, *Love: A Question for Feminism in the Twenty-first Century*. New York: Routledge, 97–111.

Jackson, S. (2015). 'Love, Social Change and Everyday Heterosexuality'. In A. G. Jonasdottir & A. Ferguson, *Love: A Question for Feminism in the Twenty- first Century*. 33–47.

Jeelani, G. (2018, 14 February). 'Delhi's Housing Plans in a Muddle'. *Hindustan Times*.

Jonasdottir, A. G. (2015). 'Love Studies: A (Re)New(ed) Field of Feminist Knowledge Interests'. In Jonasdottir & Fergusaon, *Love: A Question for Feminism in the Twenty-first Century*. 11–30.

Kakar, S. & Chowdhry, K. (1970). *Conflict and Choice: Indian Youth in a Changing Society*. Bombay: Somaiya Publications Pvt Ltd.

Mehrotra, D. P. (2001). 'Beyond the Stereotypes of "Masculine" Violence and "Feminine" Silence'. *Psychological Foundations* (Issue theme: Violence), 6–9.

Migiliaccio, T. (2009). 'Men's Friendships: Performances of Masculinity'. *The Journal of Men's Studies* 17: 3, 226–41.

Mishra, P. K. (2015, 27 Feburary). 'How Social Media is Transforming Indian Politics'. Retrieved 4 January 2018, from World Economic Forum. Available at: https://www.weforum.org/agenda/2015/02/how-social-media-is-transforming-indian-politics/

Morrow, V. (2011). 'Rethinking Childhood Dependency: Children's Contributions to the Domestic Economy'. *Sociological Review* 44: 1, 58–79.

Morrow, V. (2013). 'Whose Values? Young People's Aspirations and Experiences of Schooling in Andhra Pradesh'. *India. Children & Society*, 27: 258–69.

Morrow, V. & Crivello, G. (2015). 'What is the Value of Qualitative Longitudinal Research with Children and Young People for International Development?' *International Journal of Social Research Methodology* 18: 3, 267–80.

National Youth Policy 2014. (2014). Retrieved 4 January 2018, from the Ministry of Youth affairs and Sports. Available at: http://www.rgniyd.gov.in/sites/default/files/pdfs/scheme/nyp_2014.pdf

Nguyen, C. (n.d.). Interpellation. Retrieved 4 January 2018, from The Chicago School of Media Theory. Available at: https://lucian.uchicago.edu/blogs/mediatheory/keywords/interpellation/

Phadke, S., Khan, S., & Ranade, S. (2011). *Why Loiter? Women & Risk on Mumbai Streets*. New Delhi: Penguin Books.

Ramalingegowda, C. (2014). 'How Indian Politicians Are Using Social Media to Build Personal Brands'. *Your Story*. Retrieved 4 January 2018. Available at: https://yourstory.com/2014/09/politicians-social-media/

Schneebaum, A. (2015). 'All in the family: Patriarchy, Capitalism and Love'. In Jonasdottir & Ferguson, *Love: A Question for Feminism in the Twenty-first Century*, 127–40.

Snell-Rood, C. (2015). *No One Will Let Her Live*. Oakland, CA: University of California Press.

Standke-Erdmann, B. (2001). 'Who Sows Wind Will Reap Storm: Structural Violence In India'. *Psychological Foundations* (Issue Theme: Violence), 30–34.

Sultan, P. (2018, 12 February). 'Three master plans, 50 years, same old Delhi'. *Hindustan Times*. Available at https://www.hindustantimes.com/delhi-news/three-master-plans-50-years-same-old-delhi/story-u0hiX5hAbS7hIrxfT-CEdQM.html

Tarlo, E. (2001). 'Welcome To History: A Resettlement Colony in the Making'. In Veronique Dupont, Denis Vital and Emma Tarlo (eds), *Delhi, Urban Spaces and Human Destinies*. New Delhi: Manohar Publishers and Distributors and Centre de Sciences Humanities. 51–71.

Walker, K. (1995). '"Always There for Me": Friendship Patterns and Expectations among Middle- and Working-class Men and Women'. *Sociological Forum*, Volume 10, 273–96.

Walker, K. (1994). 'Men, Women and Friendships: What they Say, What they Do'. *Gender and Society, Volume 8*, 246–65.

Wellman, B , Carrington, P. & Hall, A. (1988). 'Networks as Personal Communities'. In Barry Wellman and S. D. Berkowitz (eds), *Social Structures: A Network Approach*. Cambridge: Cambridge University Press. 130–84.

About the Author

Nirantar Trust is a non-profit organization that has been working in the fields of gender, education and the democratic rights movement over the last two decades. They are an active part of the women's movement in India and draw their values from feminist principles. They are firmly rooted in community-based work which informs their research and advocacy too.

Nirantar works with feminist pedagogy and practices to develop collective knowledge and resources about the lives of women in India. They make direct field interventions, build capacities, develop feminist leadership, create educational resources, and conduct research and advocacy deeply rooted in the lives of marginalized girls and women.

Restless in the City has emerged from a collective of feminist researchers and advocacy specialists. It was led by Ekta Oza and Sonam Grover with the guidance of Dr Sarada Balagopalan, Associate Professor of Childhood Studies at Rutgers University, Camden.